THE

JOY OF

COSTCO

THE JOY OF COSTCO

A TREASURE HUNT
FROM A to Z

WRITTEN BY
DAVID & SUSAN SCHWARTZ

DESIGNED BY EIGHT AND A HALF

HOT DOG PRESS, LLC
NEW YORK

Hot Dog Press, LLC
163 Amsterdam Avenue, #1220
New York, NY 10023

www.HotDogPress.LLC

For information, contact Hot Dog Press, LLC
163 Amsterdam Avenue, #1220, New York, NY 10023

First Edition, September 2023

ISBN: 978-1-959-50500-6

Library of Congress Control Number: 2023907586

Manufactured in the United States by
Lakeside Book Company

Design by Bonnie Siegler and Andrew James Capelli
www.8point5.com

Illustrations by Martin Hargreaves

Edited by Ron Brawer

For Our Parents ♡

HELEN & RAY AND
MEL & MARILYN

WHOSE LOVE OF PRICE CLUB
AND COSTCO STARTED US ON
THIS JOURNEY…

TABLE OF CONTENTS

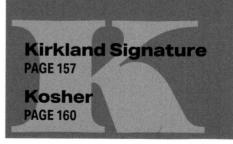
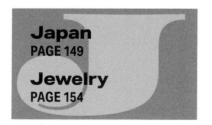

PROLOGUE

We live in one of the smallest apartments in NYC, and yet we are two of the biggest fans of Costco in the world.

"Costco."

DAVID & SUSAN SCHWARTZ, SAN DIEGO, JUNE 2018

This book was sparked by a desire to travel the world and find out more about what Susan describes as her "happy place": vast warehouses filled with an ever-changing array of top-quality products at rock-bottom prices. There were just two problems: Covid made travel a challenge and Costco management was not keen on the idea of a book. Please note that this book was neither authorized nor financed by Costco. Many past and current employees helped us, but we wrote this entirely on our own.

Our NYC apartment is only 450 square feet, so we don't have a lot of room for storage. Still, whenever we travel, we always visit the local Costco and can't resist bringing things back with us. As we go to

press in May 2023, there are over 850 Costco warehouses worldwide and we have been to over 200 of them. There are four US states without a single Costco warehouse: Maine, Rhode Island, West Virginia, and Wyoming. We plan to visit *at least* one Costco warehouse in every other state in the Union that has one (plus Washington, DC and Puerto Rico) and *at least* one Costco warehouse in thirteen other countries: Australia, Canada, China, France, Iceland, Japan, Mexico, New Zealand, South Korea, Spain, Sweden, Taiwan, and the United Kingdom.

Even though Costco management remains steadfastly humble and doesn't really want a book written, we were given behind-the-scenes looks at depots, packaging facilities,

HOT DOG TASTING, ILLINOIS, FEBRUARY 2022

vendors, a pre-opening party for employees and vendors, and a meat processing plant. We are eternally grateful to co-founder Jim Sinegal for reviewing our manuscript.

Our goal: to write a fan book that shares our appreciation of the company with our fellow Costco enthusiasts (members, employees, vendors, and shareholders alike). It's not easy, but Costco does the right thing even when no one is looking — and still makes money. It requires hard work, discipline, and dedicated employees.

The pages ahead will take you on a whirlwind trip around the globe, looking at every aspect of this unique retailer, from logistics and merchandising to quality control

and warehouse openings. We hope you will marvel, as we did, learning about this 40-year-old company. Did you know that Costco is the largest importer of olive oil and cashews in the world? That it sells *seven times* more hot dogs than all MLB stadiums *combined?* Or that when Costco changed its source of salmon from Chile to Norway it impacted the economies of *both* countries? Or that Costco sells six million pumpkin pies each year, but only between September and December?

We've organized the book alphabetically, in part to replicate the seemingly random experience of shopping at Costco, with the feeling of a Treasure Hunt, never knowing what's in the next aisle — or section of the book. Under "C," for example,

you'll find "Chicken" and "China"; under "P," explore "Parking Lots" and "Pumpkin Pie." The Q&A format is designed to be engaging and make the experience fun and informative. Dip in wherever you like and enjoy — just as you would in a Costco warehouse!

Even though this is a fan book, we haven't shied away from pointing out what some might perceive as missteps along the way. For example, it took Costco longer to switch to cage-free eggs than was vowed in 2006 (which drew ire from animal rights activists and two celebrities, Brad Pitt and Ryan Gosling). Nor has every warehouse been a success. Costco was met with disinterest in the Midwest in the early years and pulled out, closing three warehouses, only

returning to the region in 1998, opening a record five warehouses in a single day.

Like Costco, we wanted to maintain quality control from beginning to end, so we set up Hot Dog Press, our own publishing company, specifically for this book. Plus, we love Costco's hot dogs.

It took us seven years working daily side by side to research, write, and publish this book — and we're still happily married! We're also still living in our tiny apartment where we've made room for this book on our coffee table. We hope you might do the same wherever you live, opening it from time to time to learn from and enjoy **The Joy of Costco: A Treasure Hunt from A to Z**.

A BRIEF HISTORY OF COSTCO

FIRST COSTCO WAREHOUSE, SEATTLE, 1983

SOL PRICE

SOL PRICE

IT ALL BEGAN WITH A MAN NAMED SOL PRICE. His parents, Sam and Bella, were Russian Jewish immigrants who both worked in the garment industry in New York. In 1916, their third child, Sol, was born in the Bronx. After his father developed tuberculosis, the family moved to San Diego, California, because New York winters were too harsh for Sam. The marriage wasn't an easy one; Bella, who was quite independent, moved back and forth across the country several times with her three children.

Sol was resilient, smart, and high energy; he graduated from college and law school at USC in Los Angeles. By then, Sol had married his high school sweetheart, Helen Moskowitz. They returned to San Diego and had two children, Robert and Larry.

At the start of World War II, Sol was declared 4F because of a droopy, partially blind left eye. Still, he wanted to do his share for the war effort, so while keeping his law practice afloat in the mornings, he worked another 12 hours a day training aircraft maintenance workers to repair B-24 heavy bombers.

In booming postwar California, Sol built a successful law practice, focused on small-scale merchants, many of whom were also Jewish.

FEDCO

MANDELL WEISS, FEDMART, SAN DIEGO

ONE OF SOL'S wartime legal clients was the Seven Seas Locker Club, an outlet in Los Angeles where, for a small membership fee, sailors on shore leave could store their uniforms, change into civvies, and buy discounted supplies for themselves and family members.

Postwar, the Seven Seas Locker Club merged with a similar war-time operation — the Post and Naval Exchanges — to form Fedco (Federal Employees' Distributing Company), a non-profit, members-only department store chain that operated in Southern California. Lifetime membership was less than five dollars. The stores sold high-quality clothing, footwear, housewares, jewelry, furniture, appliances, sporting goods, hardware, toys, electronics, and produce — all at very low prices, but only to federal employees.

In late 1953, Sol was faced with a problem: what to do with a warehouse his mother-in-law inherited, which was in an industrial area near San Diego Bay. Initially he rented the space to various jewelry merchants, including Leo Freedman and Mandell Weiss, who had started a company called Four Star Jewelers and were looking to expand. Searching for a more robust use of the space, Sol, Leo, and Mandell drove to Los Angeles to visit Fedco.

The trio was so impressed with the operation that they approached Fedco about setting up a franchise in the San Diego warehouse.

Fedco refused.

SOL WAS FACED WITH A PROBLEM: WHAT TO DO WITH A WAREHOUSE HIS MOTHER-IN-LAW INHERITED.

FEDMART

FEDMART, SAN DIEGO

IN 1954, REBUFFED BY FEDCO, Sol, Leo, and Mandell started FedMart (Federal Employees Merchandise Mart) which, like Fedco was not-for-profit, but had a separate profit-based purchasing and distribution arm called Loma Supply Corporation. Ten partners invested $5,000 each for a total initial investment of $50,000. They brought along a young man named Larry Bertrand, whom Leo and Mandell had hired, to help out.

Leo served as the first president of FedMart, with Larry doing a lot of the legwork. Indeed, some early FedMart alumni give Larry major credit for the successful launch. Over time, Sol took more of a leadership role, succeeding Leo as president, and shaping the business according to his own principles.

Sol hated the term "discount," because it implied low quality — he was always careful to use the term "low margin." Uniquely, Sol considered himself a fiduciary for his customers at FedMart, as he had with his clients in his law practice. For Sol, business was about more than making money; it was a social contract with his customers and the communities in which he operated. Sol was not just a lawyer and merchant; throughout his life, his charitable contributions were quietly very significant.

The first FedMart, located at 2380 Main Street in downtown San Diego, was an immediate success. Open only to members of the military or government employees, it charged a modest two dollars for a lifetime membership. It was also a stark departure from local department stores. While department stores were fancy and high service, FedMart was no-frills and low-touch, selling high-quality goods at reduced prices with minimal sales assistance. It offered products in a wide range of categories, but with a strict limit on the number of choices in each category. Sol later dubbed this the "intelligent loss of sales." If customers wanted an item badly enough, they would buy it in bulk and, if not, Sol was willing to lose the sale. By limiting the markup on goods, Sol increased sales volume and built trust with his customers. Many of the sales departments at FedMart started as concessions, with space rented to outside merchants selling items like furniture, jewelry, and children's clothing, but they were bought out early on to unify the merchandising strategy throughout the store. Significantly, FedMart sold no fresh or frozen food.

The membership component of FedMart helped Sol circumvent the fair trade laws which were enacted in the late 1930s as a form of price protection for the dominant retailers. He abhorred these laws, because they artificially kept prices above a certain floor, preventing him from charging what he considered a fair price. For example, Sol charged only $345 for a 13-inch RCA TV, even though RCA wanted merchants to charge $399. Soon after an RCA rep saw this low price at a FedMart, RCA decreed that TVs could not be sold below $399 in Imperial or San Diego County, which were the specific locations in which FedMart

BY LIMITING THE MARKUP ON GOODS, SOL INCREASED SALES VOLUME AND BUILT TRUST WITH HIS CUSTOMERS.

was operating. In retaliation, Sol placed an ad in select southern California newspapers explaining that RCA was insisting he sell their televisions at $50 over the price FedMart wanted to charge, and that RCA had specifically targeted FedMart because of its pricing.

Not surprisingly, RCA withdrew its demands.

Sol's objection to the fair trade laws led him to create FM, a line of private label goods. The fair trade laws, supported by the big liquor brands, only pertained to resale and were intended to protect brand equity; since private label liquor was not a resale, the laws did not apply. In the 1970s, the fair trade laws on many items were lifted, but they still applied to hard liquor, and FedMart was forced to sell low-price spirits under its private label brand because it could not sell branded spirits below the legal floor. In 1975, when Congress repealed the fair trade laws nationally — with the exception of liquor — Sol immediately challenged the California liquor law by selling nationally branded liquor at FedMart at only 12% above cost, the same as his private label liquor and well below the floor set by California law. Major liquor manufacturers sued him, but he won, arguing that Nixon's 1971 wage and price controls prevented him from charging a higher markup. That was the decisive blow to fair trade laws in California.

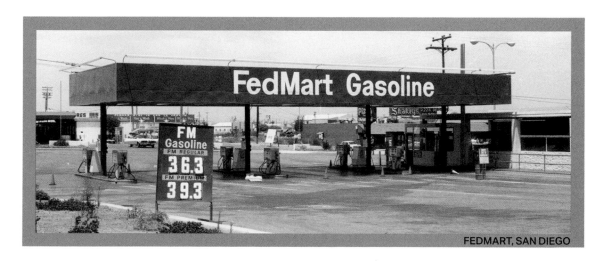

FEDMART, SAN DIEGO

CORE VALUES

FEDMART, TEMPE, ARIZONA

SOL WAS FAIR to his employees and vendors. Once, to increase sales of a ladies' hosiery product, he convinced the manufacturer to reduce the price from $3.99 to $2.99. Sol offered to share any increase in profits with the vendor. When sales didn't increase as expected, he restored the price to $3.99 and returned the lost profit to the vendor, because it was the right thing to do.

FedMart was based on four basic principles, from which Sol never veered: 1) sell excellent products at the lowest possible prices, delivering value to customers; 2) offer good wages and benefits to employees; 3) adhere strictly to honest business practices; and 4) provide investors a good return on their investment. For example, when FedMart began selling gasoline, the price of its *premium* grade was lower than what most gas stations charged for *regular*.

FedMart was proud of its low pricing, but if a competitor was able to charge a lower price for an item, Sol would send his customers to the competitor.

The return policy at FedMart was also ground-breaking: anything could be returned at any time, including the membership, for a full refund.

Sol pioneered what he called the "Six Rights" of merchandising: the right thing, in the right place, at the right time, in the right quantity, in the right condition, and at the right price. He also applied this formula to people and facilities.

About a year after the first FedMart opened, Sol began to expand, first to Phoenix, and then to other parts of the American Southwest. Sol joked that it cost only $50,000 to open the first store because he had no idea what he was doing; five years later and far more experienced, it cost $5 million.

As FedMart grew, Sol attracted talented people and promoted from within. Among the first was an eighteen-year-old named Jim Sinegal, who began working part-time at FedMart in December 1954 for $1.25 per hour to make extra cash while in college. Jim's first encounter with Sol was not auspicious: Jim was carrying a mattress when Sol gruffly told him to put it down before he hurt himself or broke something in the store. Ultimately one of Sol's most successful protégés, Jim rose through the ranks from grocery bagger to senior executive.

Sol's cousin Rick Libenson was also eighteen when he joined the team, in 1960. He became a brilliant merchandiser, and also worked his way up to senior executive.

Both Jim and Rick continued to work with Sol for many years.

Having repaired airplane engines during the war, Sol always worried about the safety of air travel. In the early days of FedMart, to check on the various stores, he and his family would never fly; they would drive from San Diego all the way to Phoenix,

San Antonio, El Paso, Houston, and back. Eventually, he bought a bus and turned it into a travelling office, taking his growing executive team on frequent road trips to visit stores. They worked during the day, and in the evenings returned to the bus to socialize and then sleep in the bus on convertible beds.

FedMart became so successful that numerous imitators sprang up around the country. At one point, a man claiming to be a California state bedding inspector arrived and asked many questions — about everything but bedding. Eventually, Sol told the man to leave, convinced that the man was spying for a competitor, but Sol also learned an important lesson. His business had to be above rebuke, able to withstand the most intense and intrusive regulatory scrutiny — as long as doing so didn't violate any of his deeply held personal beliefs. For example, in Texas in 1957, to circumvent the Jim Crow requirement for segregated seating, the food court in San Antonio had only standing tables where anyone could eat. The next year, Sol refused to segregate the bathrooms in Dallas.

Early on, Sol genially gave an extensive FedMart tour to a young man named Sam Walton, who then went on to open, in Arkansas, the first of his many WalMart stores.

FedMart paid its employees the same wage in Arizona and Texas as in California, despite the lower cost of living. Sol's philosophy was that they were doing the same job and were therefore entitled to the same wage.

In 1959, FedMart went public, with five locations, $26 million in sales, and $470,000 in annual profit. As the enterprise continued to grow, it added several important ancillary businesses: pharmacy, optical, and hearing centers.

By the late 1960s, within four years of joining his father in the business, Robert Price was promoted to Senior Vice President of Operations. Robert continued his father's tradition of treating employees well.

When faced with a secondary boycott by a bakers' union, instead of breaking the strike Robert opted to address the union's concerns.

In 1969, Sol switched his sourcing for grapes from a non-union supplier to United Farm Workers, even though the price was higher. Two years later, he featured civil rights activist Cesar Chavez in a print ad for FedMart's private label FM cola.

FedMart also opened two distribution centers which sold merchandise to the stores at a very small markup and provided for centralized control of merchandise. Jim Sinegal became the executive in charge of these operations, which were critical in helping keep down costs. In California, employees at the distribution center were members of the Teamsters Union (workers in the store were members of the Retail Clerks Union); Arizona, New Mexico, and Texas were all right-to-work states and so the employees were not union members.

1. SELL EXCELLENT PRODUCTS AT THE LOWEST POSSIBLE PRICES, DELIVERING VALUE TO CUSTOMERS

2. OFFER GOOD WAGES AND BENEFITS TO EMPLOYEES

3. ADHERE STRICTLY TO HONEST BUSINESS PRACTICES

4. PROVIDE INVESTORS A GOOD RETURN ON THEIR INVESTMENT

Sol was an ideas man and he had lots of them. Some of his ideas, such as FedMart, were brilliant, others not so much. Once, he decided that FedMart would sponsor a summer evening revival of vaudeville, long dead, in San Diego's Balboa Stadium. Not surprisingly, few bought tickets. On the day of the performance the weather was so hot they couldn't even give tickets away. But if one idea failed, Sol was always onto another. It was his genius to always look for new ways to do things, make money, and make people's lives a bit easier.

"YOU'RE FIRED"

HUGO MANN

IN 1975, a young German named Hans Schoepflin, the mergers and acquisitions director for German supermarket chain Wertkauf, was traveling in the US and discovered FedMart. He returned to Germany and suggested to Hugo Mann, Wertkauf's CEO, that his company should merge with FedMart.

Mann invited Sol and Robert to Germany, where they negotiated the deal. The Prices returned to San Diego confident about the future of their company. Things turned sour over the next few months, however, and what began as a merger ended as an acrimonious buyout. Although Mann had been charming and agreeable during the merger talks, after the merger he became critical of Sol's performance and FedMart's operations. Sol was equally critical of Mann and his team, and at one point even insisted that the entire Wertkauf board resign.

On December 5, 1975, things came to a head and Sol was unceremoniously fired at a board meeting, on the grounds that he wasn't following direction. That evening, Mann changed the locks on Sol's office.

THE FEDMART STORY ENDED SADLY AND BADLY.

Robert and his brother Larry both stayed on for another week or so, but then resigned. Sol's cousin Rick Libenson, who was very loyal to Sol, also left. The FedMart story ended sadly and badly: Mann ran the business into the ground. By 1982, FedMart was closed. However, the young Schoepflin was so taken by the Prices that he stayed in the US and continued to work with them for many years and later played a role in the founding of Costco.

SOL AND ROBERT PRICE

STARTING OVER

EVER RESILIENT, Sol dusted himself off, rented the office directly above the one he had just been locked out of, and made his next move.

Although they were unsure what their new venture would be, Sol and Robert started the Price Company. They soon settled on a warehouse club retail business model with a $25 annual membership fee, which would help keep the prices as low as possible and would also incentivize members to buy enough to justify the fee.

Rick Libenson was appointed Executive Vice President for Merchandising, and Robert, President of the company, went about finding a suitable location. He found an abandoned, bare-bones, 102,000 square foot warehouse, once used as an aircraft manufacturing facility, at 4605 Morena Boulevard in the Rose Canyon section of San Diego. They bought and remodeled it, first evicting the pigeons that had taken to roosting in the beams. On July 12, 1976, with $2.5 million of capital from friends and family, they opened the first Price Club.

The idea was to serve small business owners on a wholesale basis only, largely because their lawyers had told them the area was not zoned for retail sales. Unfortunately, the first few months were a struggle; persuading small business owners to change their distributors and cast their lots with Price Club turned out to be far more difficult than the Prices anticipated. Believing they were restricted by law from retail sales, the company faced imminent disaster. At one point, Sol even instructed his employees to park near the front entrance so it would be obvious the warehouse was open for business.

Fortunately, their luck was about to change.

There was an athletic club near the warehouse at which members of the Price Club executive team would play racquetball after work, often joined by their friend and former colleague Jim Sinegal. After the Hugo Mann/Wertkauf disaster, Jim had stayed behind at FedMart for another year-and-a-half because he felt a responsibility to the thousands of employees still at the company.

One day Jim noticed that the health club was selling racquetball merchandise: racquets, balls, and athletic clothing. Yet, it was just down the street from Price Club. He pointed this out to Rick and suggested that perhaps the area was indeed zoned for retail business. Rick spoke to Robert, who in turn questioned the lawyers; but the lawyers still insisted that Price Club could not sell retail at their location. Robert went downtown himself to look at the zoning records.

It turned out the lawyers were wrong. There were no restrictions on retail business activities in the Rose Canyon area.

PRICE CLUB, SAN DIEGO, CA

WITH THE DECISION to open membership to retail customers, Price Club soared from an initial loss of $750,000 in the first year to a profit of more than $1 million, with 900 employees and 200,000 members within three years. The Prices expanded the company, first in the American Southwest, as they had with FedMart, then throughout California. The company was a huge success, driven by Sol's energy and retail flair as Chairman of the Board, Robert's operational skill and attention to detail as President, and the retailing genius and hard work of a great team, including Giles Bateman as CFO, Rick Libenson as the senior executive for merchandising, and Controller Mitch Lynn, ultimately promoted to President of The Price Company.

Sol had very strong convictions about merchandising and retailing ranging from the ideal height of a merchandise display (54 inches maximum) and aisle width (six feet) to the importance of straight, clean, and neat tops of merchandise displays. He was a demanding taskmaster, whom Jim once described as "shoe leather on the outside, but a marshmallow inside." Sol was tough but always fair, charitable, and extremely loyal. For him, business was about more than making money: doing the right thing was sacrosanct. That legacy lives on to this day at Costco.

As Price Club grew, the number of stockholders increased until it exceeded 500, which forced the company to list with the SEC and go public, which it did on July 12, 1980, its fourth anniversary.

When the Price Club's audited financials were filed, as required in the process, other retailers began to take notice — Sol was making a lot of money and doing it on his own unique terms.

In November 1982, Joe Ellis, a top-rated Goldman Sachs analyst, published a report on Price Club, which circulated widely and raised considerable interest in the warehouse club operation. In the report, he called attention to the key elements of Price Club's business model: restricted number of SKUs (Stock Keeping Units); radical stripping of expenses in the logistics chain; efficient and fast turnover of inventory; discipline to keep prices as low as possible; and the cushion provided by membership fees. He also predicted the growth of this retail channel nationwide due to the business model's strong fundamentals.

AS MANY AS 25 PRICE CLUB CLONES POPPED UP IN THE NEXT FEW YEARS.

It was an eye-opener to anyone who read it and inspired many to jump into the business. To this day, Joe remains as modest about his influence in sparking the growth of this sector as the company about which he was writing. As many as 25 Price Club clones popped up in the next few years. While most of them failed or ended up being bought by larger retailing conglomerates, one, based in the Pacific Northwest, was destined to outlast even Price Club.

COSTCO

JEFF BROTMAN AND JIM SINEGAL

WHEN PRICE CLUB went public, a young Seattle lawyer named Jeff Brotman, who split his time between a law practice and various retail interests with his father and brother, was traveling in France. He became enamored with the French retailer Carrefour, a vast warehouse grocery store — a *hypermarché*. When Jeff returned to the US, his father mentioned the Price Club phenomenon. As a result, Jeff approached the Prices with an offer to franchise a Price Club warehouse in Seattle.

The Prices showed little interest. Much as Fedco had opted not to work with Sol when he wanted to set up shop in San Diego, Sol and Robert spurned Jeff's offer.

Undaunted, Jeff began to plan his own venture, based on the Price Club model. He needed help, though, because he had never done a comparable retail venture, and began looking for Price Club alumni who would be willing to partner with him. He cold-called Rick Libenson, who explained that he was still deeply involved with Price Club and was also Sol's cousin, so he wasn't interested. However, Rick suggested Jim Sinegal, the man who'd noticed the retail racquetball shop near the Rose Canyon warehouse.

FROM THE BEGINNING JIM AND JEFF GOT ALONG VERY WELL.

Beginning in 1977, Jim sojourned briefly at Price Club as Executive Vice President of Operations, but had left a little over a year later and joined forces with Ken Chamberlin to form a brokerage and sales representative service for vendors trying to place their products in big box stores like Price Club. He often received calls from people who wanted to replicate the Prices' success. He always listened politely as he felt that contacts like these might someday come in handy, but nothing had yet clicked.

When Jeff called, Jim reacted the same way, willing to talk because he might eventually do business with him. Jeff had a vacation home in Palm Springs and offered to fly down from Seattle to meet Jim there. Jim lived in Orange County, California, which meant a two-hour drive to Palm Springs just for a meeting. But Jeff was persuasive.

FIRST COSTCO WAREHOUSE, SEATTLE, 1983

On his drive to Palm Springs, Jim got a speeding ticket, his third one that week, two of which were from the same officer. "This is not your week," the officer noted as he handed the future Costco CEO the second ticket. That traffic cop had no idea how wrong he was! Jeff later teased Jim that the only reason he agreed to leave California was because of all his speeding tickets.

From the beginning the two men got along very well, although they were from very different backgrounds and had very different senses of personal style. Jeff, born in Washington State, was Jewish, loved sports cars (he drove a lime-green Porsche convertible in the 1970s), and dressed elegantly. Tall and slim, he was the 1978 Washington racquetball champion in both singles and doubles.

Jim was born in Pittsburgh where he swam in the Allegheny River as a young kid and moved to California for high school. He was Catholic, the son of a steelworker. Physically he was a contrast to Jeff: shorter and stockier, with an impressive moustache in his later years. Jim was not a flashy dresser. Together, they resembled a modern day version of the comic book characters Mutt and Jeff. Despite their apparent differences, they shared a great sense of humor — and a passion for business.

The first meeting went well, and they scheduled more meetings, with the entire Brotman family eventually moving to Palm Springs for several months while the two men developed the business plan for a brand new wholesale entity to rival Price Club.

It would be called Costco.

The plan they drew up included a copy of the Joe Ellis/Goldman Sachs report, which the young Hans Schoepflin had passed to Jim and which they viewed as a blueprint for their new company. To this day, Jim is quick to acknowledge they were not trying to be geniuses, they just wanted to clone Price Club's winning formula, which they knew and respected.

They considered different locations for the new business, including Dallas, Chicago, and Colorado, but not California, despite the state's sizeable population, because they did not want to battle Price Club on its home turf. Ultimately, they selected Jeff's hometown of Seattle since it was in the same time zone as Jim's home in Orange County, with numerous daily flights back and forth, and it was one of the least competitive retail locations in the country, dominated by high priced vendors like Safeway.

Another reason to choose Seattle: Jeff expected a fair portion of the initial funding to come from Seattle-based investors. Jeff and Jim did the fundraising themselves rather than hiring bankers. Financiers Fred Paulsell and John Meisenbach helped them raise money from a network of friends and family. Their initial business plan was to open twelve warehouses in the Pacific Northwest earning $80 million per store annually with a goal of becoming a $1 billion company. Investors offered $3.5 million more than they needed, but the Costco team didn't want to change the offering documents, so they simply returned the extra money. Crucially, they had no exit strategy: they planned to run the business as far as it would go.

JIM AND JEFF DEVELOPED THE BUSINESS PLAN FOR A BRAND NEW WHOLESALE ENTITY TO RIVAL PRICE CLUB.

During the first few months of working on the business plan, Jim was somewhat reluctant to commit fully to the project. He had lived in southern California his entire adult life, his family was there, and he wasn't jazzed about trading sunny Orange County for rainy Seattle. Before they started raising money, however, Jim had fully committed himself to the venture. Once fundraising was completed, they leased a warehouse on 4th Avenue South, in the industrial section of Seattle, and began hiring personnel.

Eager to get a running start, they formed a small senior management team, gathering people who had previously worked with Jim, who had deep experience in warehouse retail and the grocery business, and who all knew each other well. Most were old FedMart alumni, willing to take a gamble on the new venture because they liked Jim and Jeff and had confidence in the business model. Several took significant pay cuts to join the team or relocated to Seattle, or both.

There were ten in all: Bernie Goldberg, head of apparel and housewares; Bob Thornberg, head of hardlines; Stan McMurray, head of food and sundries; Bob Craves, head of membership and marketing; Hamm Clark, head of finance; Dick DiCerchio, head of operations and warehouse selection; Leo Rogers, manager of the first warehouse in Seattle; Tom Walker, manager of the warehouse in Portland; Court Newberry, manager of the Spokane warehouse; and Tim Rose, hired as a warehouse manager for future expansion. By Spring 1984, they were joined by FedMart alums Franz Lazarus, Craig Jelinek, and Joe Portera. This team, with the exception of Hamm Clark who left in 1985, were the founding officers responsible for the company's future success. (Richard Galanti, a young man on the Donaldson, Lufkin, & Jenrette team that managed the second round of financing, was also hired in spring 1984, and in 1985 replaced Clark as CFO. Galanti is still with Costco.)

On September 15, 1983, within six weeks of leasing the space, the first Costco Wholesale warehouse opened.

While they were getting ready to open, a lawyer they had retained advised them that they should reach out to a union to organize the workforce. Jim and Dick approached the Teamsters, who were probably stunned to be invited to the warehouse. Teamsters representatives spent about a week in the warehouse and then vanished. When Jim noticed that they had stopped coming, he called the union's Seattle headquarters. Officials there explained that Costco employees simply showed no interest in unionizing.

Initially, Jim commuted between Orange County and Seattle, returning to California every weekend. His two older children were already away at college, but his daughter was still in high school and didn't want to leave her friends. Although his wife Janet tried to reassure her that the family would never leave

California, Jim proved her wrong and in the summer of 1983 they moved to Seattle. It took their daughter two years to forgive him.

Many years later, when asked if he knew Costco was going to be so successful, Jeff would say with a twinkle in his eye that he always knew it was going to be big, but that his wife, Susan, lacked his vision. She had been an executive at Nordstrom's, an upscale department store based in Seattle, and balked when Jeff said he planned to sell high-end merchandise in a bare-bones warehouse: "It'll never work," she claimed, but later gladly admitted she was wrong.

The business was a direct copy of the Price Club model. Members would pay an annual fee to shop. Costco would sell carefully curated, high-quality items with a low mark-up in large, no-frills warehouses. Like Price Club, the new company would treat employees with respect and promote from within, but would pay them even better. Costco would also treat vendors with respect, knowing they too had to make a profit, but insisting on the lowest possible prices so the savings could be passed to members. They would strip down internal costs and look for efficiencies wherever possible to create additional savings for members and decent wages for employees. The Prices had proven that this was a winning business model. Jim and Jeff now set out to demonstrate that they too could make it work.

That first Costco warehouse was almost a catastrophe. Soon after they signed the lease, Jim and Jeff were informed by the city that the 4th Avenue South Bridge, the main artery linking the warehouse district to the city, would be closed indefinitely for repairs. Worse yet, the date set for closure was five days before the warehouse was scheduled to open. Jim pleaded with the city planners, but the best they could offer was a two-week window before work would begin, because there'd been a delay in the arrival of the building supplies.

In a stroke of very bad luck for the city, but very good luck for Costco, the lights ordered for the bridge turned out to interfere with air traffic coming into nearby Boeing Field, so the city had to order new ones, delaying the bridge closure for an additional two months. By the time the bridge eventually closed, Costco shoppers were willing to take any route necessary to get to the warehouse. Costco's founders were always cognizant of and grateful for the role that luck played in the company's success.

JIM AND JEFF WERE ALWAYS AWARE OF THE ROLE LUCK PLAYED IN COSTCO'S SUCCESS.

PENTAGON CITY, ARLINGTON, VIRGINIA

THE WAREHOUSE WARS

JIM AND JEFF, ANCHORAGE COSTCO, 1984

DESPITE A TEMPORARY GLITCH on Costco's opening day, when the cash registers stopped working and all sales had to be recorded by hand, sales doubled every week, so Jim and Jeff decided to go for another round of funding to help them expand more quickly. Their hands full with their booming business, they opted to use a team of young bankers from Donaldson, Lufkin, & Jenrette, led by Hamilton "Tony" James.

When the Prices realized what was happening, they were not happy. Jim had been a loyal lieutenant in the old FedMart days and during his short stint at Price Club. They were even less happy, when by the end of 1983, Costco had quickly opened two more warehouses — in Portland, Oregon, and Spokane, Washington — establishing beachheads in territories that were already under threat from Salt Lake City-based Price Savers, one of the other newly formed competitors.

Ken Chamberlin, Jim's former consulting partner, had been briefed by Price Savers about their plans to establish a Northwest presence — in Seattle,

Tacoma, and Anchorage — because they knew the information would get back to Jim. The diversion backfired; instead of scaring the partners off, Costco sped up plans to open in those locations to beat Price Savers to the punch.

A period of intense competition between Price Club and Costco followed, as the two companies branched out across the continent, fighting each other — and the many other new competitors spurred on by Joe Ellis's report — for market share and profits. Costco opened in western Canada; Price Club started operations in Quebec. Costco moved into Florida and Price Club to Mexico as the competition raged on in North America over the next decade.

Costco's initial forays were not uniformly successful. The Salt Lake City opening, for example, was initially a disappointment, perhaps because the local community, predominantly Mormon, was already well served by Mormon-owned Price Savers. (Ironically, one of Costco's Salt Lake City locations is now the largest in the world, with about 230,000 square feet of floor space.) Warehouses in Milwaukee, Minneapolis, and Tampa did not work out either, so Costco decided to close them, but eventually came back to all of these cities.

By the early 1990s, Costco had the edge over Price Club in momentum. The combination of Jim and Jeff was magic. Both were inspirational, charismatic leaders and they had complementary skill sets. Jeff was a visionary with a knack for strategy and for selecting great warehouse locations. Jim focused on merchandising, operational detail, and efficiency. With a superb management team around them, they were unstoppable.

The Prices faced other problems that had little to do with the competition. Sol was getting older and leaving most of the day-to-day business to Robert. More significantly, tragedy struck in 1989, when Robert's 15-year-old son Aaron died of cancer. In the wake of this tragedy, Sol and Robert decided to sell their company to a strategic buyer. They considered various possibilities but kept coming back to the obvious solution: a merger with Costco. Although they were fierce competitors, the two companies shared a common DNA and core values.

THE RESULT WAS A RETAILING POWERHOUSE WITH 195 WAREHOUSES IN THE US, CANADA, AND MEXICO.

Negotiations began in early 1993. The process was fraught; meetings often ended abruptly and with animosity. Rick Libenson, who watched from the sidelines as the two parties bickered, once heard that Jeff had walked away from the talks. Rick called Jeff from a pay phone to urge him to return to the table.

Fortunately, every time the negotiations faltered the two parties found a way to get back on track. The fact is, a merger made sense for both companies. In a 2016 panel discussion with Jim, Jeff, and Rick, Robert recalled that deciding to merge with Costco was the toughest decision he ever had to make, but that it was the right one. By June 1993, the Price Company and Costco agreed to merge under the name PriceCostco with a stock swap valued at more than $2 billion. Robert would serve as Chairman, Jeff accepted the role of Vice Chairman, and Jim would be CEO of the merged entity. The result was a retailing powerhouse with 195 warehouses in the US, Canada, and Mexico, about $16 billion in annual sales, and two separate headquarters: Price Club in San Diego, Costco in Seattle.

Merging the two companies was a monumental challenge. Not only did the two management teams need to be integrated up and down the line, but operations had to be unified. It took a while to persuade people who had been aggressive competitors to work together toward the same goals. Initially, employees would ask each other at the newly merged company "Are you red (Costco) or blue (Price Club)?" but over time, employees accepted that they were now working for one company. The fact that the two companies had very similar working cultures was perhaps the only thing that made it possible. In an effort driven by founding team member Tom Walker, the company began to streamline logistics and develop the cross-docking depots and processes that formed the basis for the way the company still works today, bringing products from vendors to members with record efficiency.

Given the dynamics between the two pairs of founders, it is not particularly surprising that the marriage didn't last long. Sol and Robert, as founders of the members-only warehouse retailing concept, were justifiably proud of what they had built and found it hard to share control with Jim and Jeff who, for their part, felt the same way about working with the Prices.

By December 1994, Sol and Robert negotiated a buy-out from Jim and Jeff, taking some of the real estate assets of the merged entity and creating a new business, Price Enterprises. The Prices continued to run a warehouse retail club in Central and South America and the Caribbean, which still operates under the name PriceSmart.

Costco did not officially change the company's name from PriceCostco to Costco Companies, Inc. until 1997, and then changed it again in 1999 to Costco Wholesale Corporation.

GWANGMYEONG, SEOUL, 2022

GLOBAL EXPANSION

AFTER THE PRICE ENTERPRISES spin-off, Jim and Jeff were free to develop the company more broadly. They were a formidable retailing team, traveling the country and the world to visit existing warehouses, getting inspiration from retailers in other countries, and exploring new regions for expansion opportunities.

One of the first things they decided was to expand globally. Prior to the merger, Costco had opened its first warehouse in western Canada in October 1985, and then two more warehouses also in the west. A year later, in 1987, Price Club followed into Canada, but opened in the east. Price Club had been in Mexico since 1992 and PriceCostco continued to expand there. Just as the merger was completed, in 1993, PriceCostco opened its first warehouse in England, in West Thurrock in Essex, an industrial area about ten miles east of London.

Costco's expansion eventually spanned the globe: South Korea (1994), Taiwan (1997), Japan (1999), Australia (2009), Spain (2014), and Iceland and France (2017). With the addition of new warehouses in China (2019), New Zealand and Sweden (2022), Costco now has a presence in thirteen countries outside the US.

Jim and Jeff's travel schedule over the years was grueling. They flew around the world, only once taking time off, when they went to visit the Great Wall and Tiananmen Square about twenty years before Costco eventually opened in China in 2019. On that earlier trip, Jim and Jeff needed the help of a potential business partner to enter China because they had visas for the Republic of China (Taiwan), not The People's Republic of China (mainland China). This was a sufficiently serious faux pas that they imagined the Chinese customs officials asking each other "How did these two clowns ever get their own plane?"

Leaving the country was much more fraught. With no explanation, they were detained at the airport by military police for several hours in a small windowless room. Feeling a bit like Laurel and Hardy on an adventure gone very wrong, Jeff broke the tension by saying to his partner "Another fine mess you've gotten us into!"

GOOD TIMES AND BAD

MOBILE, ALABAMA, 2021

IN THE EARLY 1980S, three warehouses, located in Milwaukee and Minneapolis, were not doing well. Jim and Jeff made the difficult decision to close Costco's Midwest division, after first refunding memberships, offering to relocate employees, and paying off all debts to vendors and suppliers.

They then focused entirely on the Western and Eastern regions of the US. Gradually, when the brand was better known and they could invest more time and money in states like Minnesota, Michigan, Wisconsin, and Illinois, they did return to the Midwest. On May 1, 1998, as a statement of renewed commitment to the area, Costco opened five warehouses in Detroit on a single day — a record for the largest simultaneous opening day.

Troubled warehouses in the Tampa Bay area also closed in the mid-to-late 1980s, but Costco returned to Clearwater in 2003 and to Tampa in 2017. Costco has had greater difficulty penetrating other parts of the South, though, where Sam Walton had a three-decade head start not only with Walmart, but with his copy of Costco — Sam's Club — which he opened after reading Joe Ellis's research report about Price Club and visiting Sol in San Diego. (Sol later teased Sam that he was owed a finder's fee for his inspiration of Sam's Club, but Sol never managed to collect.) There are sixteen Costco warehouses in Georgia, most in the Atlanta area, but only one in Arkansas, four in Alabama, three in Louisiana, one in Mississippi, and six in Tennessee. The single Costco in Kentucky is really in the suburbs of Cincinnati. In contrast, hundreds of Walmart stores dot the southern tier.

In the 1990s, Sam Walton showed up in Seattle and asked for a meeting with Jim and Jeff. Over breakfast, he offered to buy Costco and fold it into Walmart. The two Costco founders explained that they enjoyed running Costco and had no interest in selling it to anybody. Walton accepted the response gracefully and never raised the matter again.

Despite an early lack of penetration in the American South, Costco's growth, as measured by warehouses built, is astounding. In 1986, there were 17 locations, by 1992 there were 100 warehouses; within five years that number had doubled.

In 2018, Costco reached a milestone of 750 warehouses around the world. The growth continued, with 847 warehouses four years later, creating ample opportunity for promotion within the company. As measured by revenues, the numbers are equally impressive: the last decade saw gross revenues grow from $97 billion to over $220 billion. In that same period, net income surged from $1.7 billion to $5.8 billion.

CHANGES

ALONGSIDE THIS AMAZING RECORD of growth, the senior management team has changed. In 2012, at age 76, Jim stepped down as CEO. The transition to his successor, Craig Jelinek, was smooth. An old FedMart colleague, Craig joined Costco in early 1984 to run the Tukwila warehouse, just south of Seattle, and moved up the ranks to President and COO before taking on the top job. Jim remained on the board and stayed closely involved with the company until his full retirement in 2018. He is still in almost daily contact with Craig.

JEFF'S LOSS WAS FELT KEENLY THROUGHOUT THE ORGANIZATION.

On a much sadder note, Board Chair Jeff Brotman passed away suddenly and unexpectedly on August 1, 2017, two months shy of his 75th birthday. Always fit and in seemingly good health, it was even more shocking that Jeff passed away on the eve of the annual international managers meeting in Seattle, for which every warehouse manager from around the world had gathered to meet for several days with top management. His loss was felt keenly throughout the organization. The memorial tribute to him, available on YouTube, is truly moving. Fortunately, Costco had a strong replacement for Jeff in Tony James, the investment banker who led the second round of funding for Costco in 1983.

JIM SINEGAL AND JEFF BROTMAN

One of the many things that Costco does exceptionally well is succession planning. Promotion from within ensures that people at the top are deeply imbued with Costco's culture, understand the business model, and will be able to carry it into the future.

In 2022, Ron Vachris, Executive Vice President for Merchandising, assumed the role of President and COO, and is expected to become only the third CEO in the company's history; he has been at the company for almost forty years and is highly capable of filling Craig's shoes, and Jim's before that. Meanwhile, Craig has presided over explosive growth, tripling net income from $1.46 billion to $5.8 billion and nearly doubling the size of Costco's global workforce from 173,000 to 304,000 employees. During his tenure, net sales have grown from $88.9 billion to $222.7 billion, and the number of warehouses has increased from 598 to 847 (FY2022). Unlike virtually every other corporate CEO, however, Craig wears a name badge that says "Craig Jelinek" and "1984," the year he joined the company.

Costco remains a company that obeys the law, consistently gives members value for their money, inspires extraordinary loyalty among employees,

CRAIG JELINEK, TEDDY BEAR, AND JIM SINEGAL

IN 2012, AT AGE 76, JIM SINEGAL STEPPED DOWN AS CEO AND CRAIG JELINEK TOOK THE TOP JOB.

treats suppliers fairly, and delivers value to shareholders. It does the right thing even when no one is looking. It's such a winning formula that it's amazing that more companies don't follow Costco's lead. To be fair, while the Costco model is simple, as Goldman Sachs analyst Joe Ellis astutely observed in 1982, it requires extraordinary discipline. There is a natural tendency on the part of retailers to raise prices when they can, thinking that they are enhancing the bottom line. Costco's leaders work hard to resist that temptation and see their mission as reducing prices wherever possible, knowing that shareholders will benefit because members will buy more merchandise. If others want to copy Costco, they may find themselves performing an unnatural act — favoring members and employees over short-term profits.

The dynamic duo of Jeff Brotman and Jim Sinegal built Costco on the foundation laid by Sol Price. Jeff taught Jim to laugh a little at problems and to never hold onto anger. Their modus operandi was to agree on important decisions, going forward only in agreement. As Jim describes it, they had some doozies of fights over the years, but nothing ever carried over to the next day and a hug always brought them back together. Jeff brought a strategic vision that was compelling, and Jim was a merchandising and operations genius. Walking into a warehouse with Jim is like going to Graceland with Elvis. He knows everyone's name and stops to say hello. Much like his mentor, Sol Price, he was a demanding boss and if things weren't right at a warehouse, no one wanted to hear "I'll be back in two weeks." Jim and Jeff flew six million miles together over the almost 35 years they worked side by side. The combination of these two leaders was retailing magic, but they remained humble about Costco's success.

COSTCO BOARD, 2009

Looking back on the history of Costco, Jim identifies ten "watershed moments" that enabled Costco to grow and prosper:

1. DECEMBER 1985. Opening warehouses in Fresno and Bakersfield in California proved that Costco could compete effectively in the state against Price Club, and gave Costco a huge market for subsequent growth.

2. JUNE 1987. The introduction of fresh food, while posing challenges of its own, greatly differentiated Costco from Price Club and other competitors.

3. MAY 1988. The development of depot operations streamlined logistics and provided a basis for the most efficient and powerful logistics system in the retail industry.

4. MAY 1991. Costco extended its pricing model to cover pharmacy operations, in the process becoming one of the lowest price sellers of prescription generic drugs.

5. MARCH 1992. The launch of the Kirkland Signature private label, one of the world's most valuable brands, paved the way for development of high-quality, low-priced products that Costco controls from production to sale.

6. SEPTEMBER 1993. The merger of Costco and Price Club doubled the business overnight, and turned two fierce competitors into an integrated company.

7. APRIL 1995. Although gasoline stations had been a fixture of FedMart, Price Club had been unable to make it work. Costco gave it one last shot, and it turned out to be a major win for the company.

8. NOVEMBER 1998. E-commerce was launched and now accounts for $10 billion of sales annually.

9. AUGUST 1999. The American Express/Costco card was introduced.

10. APRIL 2000. The introduction of the Executive Membership level gave members a 2% rebate on items bought in the warehouse, which provided an option for members who were willing to pay a little more in membership fees for the extra cash back at year end.

If you ask any of the early members of the Costco team why the company has been such a success, everyone will tell you it was hard work...and a lot of luck. They will also point to the culture of integrity and the commitment to members and employees that made the difference, which can be traced directly to Sol Price, who embodied the culture that passed from generation to generation since the days of FedMart.

This unique approach to business is still in effect at Costco. For example, Costco's continuing policy of members being able to return any item at any time for a full refund is best illustrated by the return of a grand piano thirteen years after it was purchased — because the member hadn't learned to play it. That member got a full refund.

WHEN A REPORTER ASKED SOL HOW IT FELT TO HAVE FATHERED THE ENTIRE WAREHOUSE CLUB INDUSTRY, HE QUIPPED, "I SHOULD HAVE WORN A CONDOM."

A reporter once said to Jim, "You must have learned a lot from Sol Price."

Jim corrected him: ""No, that's not correct. I learned *everything* from Sol."

RON VACHRIS AND CRAIG JELINEK, 2023

A TO Z

THE
SMALLEST
COSTCO
WAREHOUSE
IN THE WORLD
IS IN
JUNEAU

ALASKA

HOW MANY COSTCO WAREHOUSES ARE THERE IN ALASKA?

There are two in Anchorage, Alaska's biggest city, and one each in Fairbanks and Juneau, the state capital. The Anchorage location was opened on October 25, 1984, after Price Saver, a Utah-based retailer, announced they were opening in Alaska; Costco moved quickly to open there first. It was only the tenth warehouse Costco ever opened. Jim Sinegal still chuckles when he recalls going to the Anchorage opening without a proper overcoat. Jeff Brotman, who also had never been to Alaska, was wearing moccasins, which made walking in the foot-deep snow a bit difficult. In terms of revenue, the first Anchorage warehouse usually ranks at the top for any warehouse in the American Northwest, second across the entire US, and third throughout the world. Combined, Anchorage's two warehouses generate more than $800 million a year in sales.

ARE THERE ANY SPECIALTY ITEMS THAT YOU WOULD FIND ONLY IN AN ALASKAN WAREHOUSE?

The most noteworthy items are blackout curtains, shrimp traps, game bags, a six-person Coleman darkroom tent, bear and pepper spray (each in a two-pack), and reindeer sausage. Local regulations prevent Costco from selling more exotic meats like moose or bear. Alaskan Bear Creek pomegranate or strawberry/rhubarb wines are popular, sold in compliance with state regulations, in a separate fenced off area in the warehouses. Alaska has no indigenous pollinators to produce honey — a key ingredient in mead, which is quite popular in The Last Frontier. Local honey is very expensive; fortunately, as of 2022, a 60-pound tub at Costco was priced at only $107.99.

WHY IS THE JUNEAU WAREHOUSE SO SMALL? HOW IS IT SOURCED?

The Juneau warehouse, nestled at the base of an enormous fir-forested mountain, is only 76,000 square feet — about 40% smaller than the average Costco warehouse. It is one of four small warehouses opened in a 1993 test program — along with ones in Kalispell, Montana, Warrenton, Oregon, and Sequim, Washington — which concluded that smaller size was not useful. (The other three have since been expanded.) Because Juneau is not accessible by land, items are brought in on fast ships by AML and Matson. Alaskan members benefit from the same prices as other US Costco members, and the produce is as fresh as that in any Seattle warehouse.

"NEVERMORE"

Savvy Alaskan Costco shoppers know to guard their groceries in the parking lot to protect against gangs of thieving ravens.

The clever birds have been known to purloin a single steak or pork chop from an unsuspecting member's cart. They're not dangerous — just hungry after a long, cold, Alaskan winter.

AUSTRALIA

**OPENING DAY SALES AT
THE FIRST AUSTRALIAN COSTCO
WERE THE HIGHEST TO DATE
FOR ANY WAREHOUSE
IN A NEW COUNTRY**

CRIKEY! THERE ARE AUSTRALIAN COSTCO WAREHOUSES?

On August 17, 2009, Costco opened in Melbourne. Costco had already expanded abroad to Canada, Mexico, the UK, and Asia: Australians had long endured high prices on imported goods, so the decision was made to establish a toehold 8,000 miles and eight time zones away from the Home Office in Issaquah, Washington. As of 2022, there were fourteen warehouses and one depot, spread around the perimeter of this vast continent. Australia has 26 million people — about two-thirds the population of Canada, a country with over 100 Costco warehouses — yet there are only fourteen in Australia to date. (Costco is working to build more.)

HOW DID COSTCO EXPAND INTO AUSTRALIA?

In the late 1990s, Don Burdick, a Costco real estate specialist, went to Australia with Jim Sinegal's son Michael to evaluate the business opportunity. In 2003, based on their report, Jim Sinegal and Jeff Brotman sent several Costco officers, including western Canada region head Hubert de Suduiraut and South Korea country manager Steve Pappas, to Australia for additional reconnaissance. Eventually, Patrick Noone, an Australian Costco executive working in Canada, returned home to select the site and supervise construction. He chose Docklands, a high-profile Melbourne location at Waterfront City, visible from the highway between the airport and the downtown area, which was undergoing a redevelopment. In keeping with the rivalry between the two cities, some in Sydney referred to the new warehouse as "a prototype," unwilling to concede that Melbourne had the first Costco warehouse.

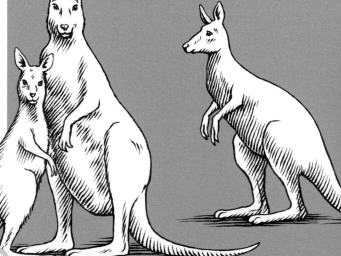

KANGA & ROO ... & ROO & ROO & ROO & ROO...

There are over 34 million kangaroos in Australia, vastly outnumbering the 26 million humans.

HOW ABOUT NOTEWORTHY ITEMS?

Australia is the only country we visited with caskets and coffins at a kiosk display near the warehouse exit (even though they are only sold online). On a brighter note, Australian warehouses sell gold bullion — such as a 500-gram bar of 24K gold for about $40,000 — manufactured by ABC, Australia's largest independent bullion dealer. Australians are very sporty, so you'll also find lots of equipment for outdoor activities such as biking, camping, water sports, and golf.

ANY SPECIAL LIQUOR?

Australians like beer and there are a good number of local and global brands. Catering to Australia's large Asian population, Costco has an assortment of Chinese grain spirits at great prices, including an aged 500-milliliter bottle of Chinese Moutai (sorghum liquor) for *only* $2,500. There are also unusual flavored and colored spirits such as Sicilian lemon gin and Japanese pink gin.

HOW IS THE FRESH AND PACKAGED FOOD DIFFERENT IN AUSTRALIA?

There's an amazing range of fresh seafood from local waters, including baby barramundi, shucked fresh Pacific oysters, and Australian bottarga. The Deli section has a lot of Asian items such as creamy Thai-style chicken soup and Korean marinated beef bulgogi. Two notable produce items are super-juicy Dracula Dekopon mandarins and the largest strawberries we've ever seen. In the rotisserie area you might find German-style pork knuckles with sauerkraut, sold in two-pound-plus packages that would easily feed a family of four. Vegemite, Australia's version of Britain's brewer's yeast extract spread Marmite, is sold in a shelf-stable two-pound tub.

ANYONE WANT TO BARBECUE?

Costco in Australia sells everything needed to barbecue, including a range of "barbies" — from a small patio deck model to huge backyard units — and wood chips, too. Australian Kirkland Signature beef is grass-fed for the majority of its life, but grain-finished for a minimum of 100 days to guarantee tender marbled flavor. The grain is different from that used in the US, where cattle are fed mostly soy and corn. In Australia, grain feed is a mixture of cereal, fiber, protein, vitamins, and minerals. Costco in Australia sells Frenched Australian lamb cutlets and plenty of shrimp, both of which are perfect for grilling.

WHAT IS ON THE MENU AT THE FOOD COURT?

Lots of stuff and it's all outstanding! The Kirkland Signature quarter-pound-plus hot dog is pork, as in the rest of the Pacific region, rather than beef. Other unique tasty items include hot clam chowder served in a bread bowl; Korean-style chicken wings; a delectable Indian-style butter chicken pie; mango or taro smoothies with or without boba (tapioca bubbles); and mini cinnamon donut balls.

AUSTRALIA
has the world's third-lowest population density — seven people per square mile — exceeded only by Mongolia and the Western Sahara.

BAKERY

THE AROMA FROM COSTO'S BAKERY GREETS YOU IN THE PARKING LOT, BEFORE YOU EVEN ENTER THE WAREHOUSE

WHEN DID COSTCO BEGIN IN-WAREHOUSE BAKERY OPERATIONS?

Costco began selling baked goods in 1987, when founding officers Stan McMurray and Tim Rose hired professional baker Sue McConnaha to start a bakery in the Seattle warehouse. Soon, Bakeries expanded throughout the system. Sue ran the business for Costco for three delicious decades and now manages Journeys, which is part of Costco's diversity and inclusion department.

WHAT HAPPENS DURING A TYPICAL DAY IN A COSTCO WAREHOUSE BAKERY?

Bakers arrive between 5-7 AM and place defrosted items, like croissants, that arrived overnight — either from the Costco baking commissary or third-party bakers — into ovens on premises. They also begin to prepare the items that are made from scratch. At 7 AM, the cake decorators and packers arrive, and fresh bread production starts. Baking continues throughout the day, with a shift change at 3 PM, when the closing team arrives and production begins to wind down. Toward the end of the day, dough is mixed and left to proof overnight, and frozen items are trayed out and placed into refrigerators to defrost. The Bakery finishes operations at about 9:30 PM — except in Japan, where some Bakeries work around the clock to keep up with demand.

STAN McMURRAY

In 1983, Jim Sinegal hired Stan McMurray as Costco's first Head Merchant, Food, and Sundries executive. Stan established regional buying teams and identified countless new suppliers.

When Stan passed away in 2016, Jeff Brotman remembered his help creating "an atmosphere of fun and challenge… [contributing to]…the company's merchandising philosophy and execution." Jim said that Costco "wouldn't be the company we are today without Stan. He was a great colleague. He had a wonderful sense of humor, and he was exceptionally good at his job."

WHAT IS THE COSTCO BAKING COMMISSARY?

In 2017, Costco's Canadian supplier of baked goods was bought by a competitor. Costco took this opportunity to build a 93,700 square foot facility in Vaughan, Ontario, northwest of Lake Ontario, to prepare baked goods for about 100 locations in Canada and 73 in the Northeast and Southeast US regions. Its four grain silos use 84,000 pounds of flour *daily*, with another silo for sugar and enough specialized equipment to produce a wide range of Kirkland Signature baked goods. During its first year, the commissary produced 600,000 croissants and multi-grain buns *every day*, with 36,000 cookies prepped and packed *per hour*.

ARE THERE REGIONAL SPECIALTIES?

In Mexico, warehouse Bakeries showcase mini-donut production in the front of the Bakeries. [SEE "MEXICO"] Japan sells a triple cheese tart with two different kinds of cream cheese and mascarpone in a pie tart shell, which can be enjoyed warm or cold. Sweden has several extraordinary baked items, including Budapest *Stubbe* — a rolled hazelnut meringue cake filled with whipped cream and tangerines — and Princess Cake *(prinsesstårta),* a traditional celebration cake with sponge cake layers, raspberry jam, and whipped cream, the whole thing encased in light green marzipan, sprinkled with powdered sugar and decorated with a pink marzipan rose.

On the books (from top):
Paul McCartney
LYRICS
A-K
L-Z

BOOKS

WHEN COSTCO DECIDES
TO SELL A BOOK,
IT CAN REPRESENT 25% OF
A BOOK'S TOTAL SALES

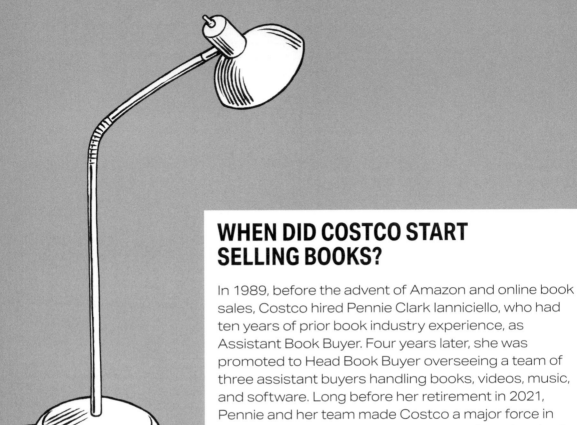

WHEN DID COSTCO START SELLING BOOKS?

In 1989, before the advent of Amazon and online book sales, Costco hired Pennie Clark Ianniciello, who had ten years of prior book industry experience, as Assistant Book Buyer. Four years later, she was promoted to Head Book Buyer overseeing a team of three assistant buyers handling books, videos, music, and software. Long before her retirement in 2021, Pennie and her team made Costco a major force in the book industry even though, at any time, they had a miniscule number of titles compared to the 30,000 carried at a typical national bookstore chain.

HOW DOES COSTCO SELECT WHICH BOOKS TO SELL?

Costco uses the same highly curated approach with books as with other products. Not all warehouses carry books, but those that do generally limit the selection of fiction, non-fiction, children's books, YA titles, cookbooks, and attractive coffee table books. The stock changes frequently as new books are published. The only criterion for book selection is whether members will like the book; Costco is neutral on politics in its literary offerings.

DOES COSTCO HAVE BOOK SIGNING EVENTS?

One of the most memorable book signings was former First Lady Michelle Obama's event for *Becoming* at the Burbank warehouse. This signing was not officially authorized, but rather an impromptu visit from Ellen DeGeneres during her morning talk show — to great comedic effect (still available on YouTube). On another occasion, former First Lady Hillary Clinton was signing books at the Pentagon City warehouse and was delighted to run into Supreme Court Justice Sonya Sotomayor. Martha Stewart regularly signed books at the Westport, Connecticut warehouse near her former home. Among others, Bill O'Reilly, Buzz Aldrin, Julie Andrews, Carol Burnett and former Presidents Jimmy Carter and Bill Clinton have also signed books at Costco.

DO OVERSEAS WAREHOUSES CARRY BOOKS?

Many overseas warehouses carry books in English and the local language. For example, the Iceland warehouse stocks books in English, because most Icelanders are fluent in English, but also sells books in Icelandic. The buying teams for non-US warehouses are regional and look for books that will appeal to their different national audiences.

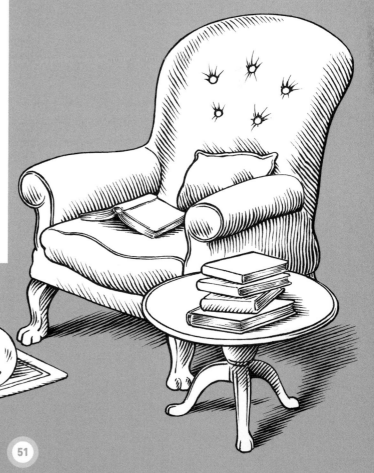

BUSINESS CENTERS

IN 2022,
COSTCO'S BUSINESS CENTERS'
314-TRUCK FLEET DROVE
ALMOST FIVE MILLION MILES
MAKING DELIVERIES

WHAT'S A COSTCO BUSINESS CENTER?

Costco Business Centers are open to all members, but are designed to meet the needs of small businesses like restaurants, corner stores, newsstands and the like with industrial equipment and larger-than-normal-even-for-Costco size packages. From the outside, Costco Business Centers may look the same as regular warehouses, but the business hours are tailored to small businesses, opening earlier and closed on Sundays. They also tend to be smaller (about two-thirds the size of a regular warehouse), have more flatbeds than carts, rarely have a Food Court, and have less parking because about half the business is fulfilled with delivery to customers. In 2022, there were 24 Business Centers in the US and six in Canada.

ARE THERE ANY OTHER DIFFERENCES BETWEEN BUSINESS CENTERS AND REGULAR WAREHOUSES?

The customer flow is about 50% lower at a Business Center (120-140 members per hour as opposed to 250-350). About 90% of the sales volume is with business owners. The end aisle displays are changed once or twice a year — versus several times per month in a regular warehouse — so shopping is more efficient and less like the Treasure Hunt experience in a standard warehouse, which offers constantly changing seasonal merchandise. The center section of a Business Center warehouse has large displays of beverages instead of apparel and there are no electronics, home décor items (including TVs and bedding), optical, or pharmacy.

COSTCO IS ALREADY KNOWN FOR BULK SHOPPING! IT GETS BIGGER STILL?

Costco's Business Centers give bulk-selling new meaning. For example, you might find a 56-gallon can of maple syrup, a five-pound plastic jar of curry powder, a three-pound container of fresh peeled garlic, or a 5½-pound container of baking powder! Costco sells sugar in 50-pound bags at all warehouses, but about 25% of it is sold at Business Centers. The vending department carries single-dose items suitable for vending machines. Some gargantuan "wow" items — like the 4½-kilo Toblerone bar we saw at the October 2022 Stockholm warehouse opening — may be sold in both Business Centers and regular warehouses.

H₂OH!

In 2016, Costco's Business Centers delivered approximately 72 million bottles of 16.9 ounce Kirkland Signature water — enough to fill the Rotunda at the US Capitol in Washington, DC!

PRODUCT SIZES IN A REGULAR COSTCO WAREHOUSE VS IN A BUSINESS CENTER		
	WAREHOUSE	**BUSINESS CENTER**
ONIONS	10 LB. BAG	50 LB. BAG
PICKLES	64 OZ. JAR	5 GAL. BUCKET
SOUR CREAM	3 LB. CONTAINER	32 LB. CONTAINER

OPENING A RESTAURANT AND NEED COMMERCIAL GRADE EQUIPMENT?

Whether you are opening a pizza parlor or simply love pizza and have a big backyard, you can buy an industrial pizza oven and have it delivered for about $25,000! You'll see professional grade gas stoves and ovens, gyro rotisseries, huge refrigerator units, and industrial mixing machines for bakeries. Professional grade pots, pans, knives, and other utensils are also available. In short, you can find everything you would need to start your own restaurant or catering service, including silverware and dishes.

WHAT ABOUT DELIVERY — OR DO I HAVE TO SCHLEP IT HOME MYSELF?

Next-day delivery is guaranteed for orders placed by 3 PM. Fulfillment crews ("pickers") — equipped with electronic finger scanners that create individual packing lists in a pre-determined order for maximum pallet packing efficiency — are busy in the warehouse from 6 PM–2 AM.

BUYING

COSTCO'S BUYING TEAMS SEARCH
OUT THE HIGHEST
QUALITY PRODUCTS AT THE
LOWEST POSSIBLE PRICES

WHAT IS COSTCO'S BUYING PROCESS?

Product selection at Costco is highly curated, more so than at other retailers: each warehouse carries no more than 3,800 Stock Keeping Units. Business Centers can have an additional 3,800 SKUs for sale online. [SEE "BUSINESS CENTERS"] The global buying team at the Seattle Home Office purchases about 60% of products — like paper towels and bottled water — to achieve the greatest economies of scale and lowest prices. Regional buying teams around the world handle the remaining 40%, which also includes seasonal items like Halloween costumes and local specialties like Marmite in the UK or Vegemite in Australia. Approximately 20% of all items are "treasure hunt" finds — items that are sufficiently special to wow a member.

WHAT IS THE PROCESS FOR SELECTING HOLIDAY TOYS?

The Home Office toy team is relatively small: a head buyer, assisted by two assistants, and two inventory control managers. The annual selection process for the following year's holiday season begins in October, when buyers send out requests to some 400 suppliers around the world. Lucky local school children are invited to play with the toys so the buyers can get feedback from the end users. In January, regional buyers gather in Seattle to review products and place orders. To optimize logistics, once final selections are made the buying team works with manufacturers to ensure that their packaging will fit on standard pallets. The end result: a colorful and fun range of toys for the holiday season.

DO BUYERS NEED SPECIAL EXPERTISE IN THEIR AREA?

Many of the buyers are generalists who, during their careers, move around within a department or even across departments, but along the way develop deep expertise in an area. In 1983, for example, Annette Alvarez-Peters joined Costco as a sales audit clerk and began buying audio and telecom products. Although Annette had no prior spirits experience, she ultimately became Costco's head liquor buyer, managing $2 billion worth of sales annually before retiring in 2020.

HOW DOES COSTCO MAINTAIN PRODUCT QUALITY?

Costco's vendors must undergo regular business audits to ensure cost-effective, high-quality manufacturing, and to be certain that Costco does not represent more than 25% of their business. Vendors also undergo social audits to confirm that their employees are treated well and the business is environmentally sound and sustainable. Costco's buyers are deeply involved in quality control: buying teams regularly visit manufacturing facilities to inspect production lines and make suggestions for quality and efficiency improvements. Cost savings are passed along to members. Costco quality assurance teams at the Home Office also test items to make sure they meet quality, safety, and regulatory standards.

COSTCO IS THE SECOND-LARGEST RETAILER IN CANADA

CANADA

WHEN DID COSTCO EXPAND INTO CANADA?

In October 1984, Costco opened in Anchorage, Alaska, over 2,000 miles from the Seattle Home Office. One year later, Costco launched in Burnaby, British Columbia, because at "only 135 miles away," it seemed like an obvious next step; two more warehouses were quickly built, also in western Canada. Jeff Brotman and Jim Sinegal thought opening in Canada was going to be the same as expanding in the US, but quickly realized that this was a major misconception. Yet, Costco Canada burgeoned from the first three warehouses to sixty-four, with former FedMart executive Ed Maron at the helm working closely with Joe Portera, who would eventually run the combined Canadian and East Coast US regions for many years. Canada now represents more than 10% of Costco's total operations, with several of the world's top-selling warehouses, and outsells Walmart with only about 25% the number of locations.

ARE THERE ANY SPECIAL ITEMS IN COSTCO'S CANADIAN BAKERIES?

Costco bakes and sells its standard Kirkland Signature bagels, but also sells commercially produced Montréal-style bagels, which are handmade, smaller, denser, have a larger hole, and are baked in a wood-fired oven. For Saint-Jean-Baptiste Day, celebrated in Québec and across Canada by French Canadians, Costco sells a fantastic layered genoise cake, decorated to look like the Québec provincial flag: vanilla icing covered in sapphire blue powdered sugar, and finished with a white fleur-de-lis. Stunning and delicious.

ANY INTERESTING NON-FOOD ITEMS?

Barbecuing, outdoor sports, and gardening are all very popular in Canada, so there is a wide range of merchandise to support these activities including, to name a few: a ton of barbecue grills, large rolls of artificial turf, and a nine-pound tub of Miracle-Gro Plant Food. If you are planning to open or run a restaurant, Costco Business Centers have you covered, with essentials like an industrial pizza oven or a 55-gallon barrel of extra virgin olive oil. The Business Centers also sell some of the same products as regular warehouses, plus a four-foot-long, 10-pound bar of Toblerone chocolate that was sadly too big for us to lug home to NYC.

DO CANADIAN WAREHOUSES SELL ANY UNUSUAL FOOD ITEMS?

Poutine — French fries topped with fresh cheese curds and gravy — is scrumptious and one of the top-selling items at Canadian Food Courts. Large bags of locally produced poutine cheese curds are also sold in freestanding refrigerator cases in the Deli. The Dairy section has a Costco-sized pack of 36 Spring Creek quail eggs from a family-owned purveyor in Saint Anns, Ontario. The fresh meat selection includes Canadian AAA beef, elk, bison, wild boar, and venison, as well as Japanese Kobe, New Zealand lamb, and Argentinian beef. Noteworthy produce items are Del Monte Pink Glow pineapples, mini-bananas from Ecuador, and fresh miniature corn from Guatemala.

WHEN DID PRICE CLUB ENTER CANADA? WHAT HAPPENED AFTER THE MERGER?

In 1987, Price Club steered clear of Costco in the west and instead set up shop in eastern Canada, led by Pierre Mignault, joined by Louise Wendling — who later became country manager for Costco. Price Club targeted mainly individual members, while Costco focused on business customers, which resulted in higher sales and greater momentum heading into the 1993 merger. The merged company maintained two separate headquarters for many years — in Laval (Price Club) and Vancouver (Costco) — only opening a new consolidated office in 2001, in Ottawa. Costco Canada remains proud of its heritage, with signs at every warehouse displaying the three different names under which the company has operated: NOUS SOMMES/WE ARE, PRICE CLUB, COSTCO WHOLESALE, COSTCO

IS IT TRUE THAT COSTCO ROTISSERIE CHICKEN STARTED IN CANADA??

In 1995, Pierre Riel and Louis Santillo, two enterprising Costco employees at Montréal's Marché Central warehouse, decided to experiment with cooking and selling fresh rotisserie chickens. The first week they sold over 6,000 chickens, which caught the attention of the Home Office. This success story has since been rolled out around the globe and the rotisserie chicken remains one of Costco's most iconic items. [SEE "CHICKEN"]

WANT TO LIVE NEAR A COSTCO?

Check out the Vancouver warehouse built underneath a luxury apartment building!

CARTS

KNOWN AS A "TROLLEY" IN
THE UK AND AUSTRALIA,
THESE WORKHORSES ARE
THE BACKBONE OF
THE SHOPPING EXPERIENCE

DOES COSTCO HAVE MOTORIZED SHOPPING CARTS?

Motorized shopping carts, which allow a shopper to remain seated, are very popular, but always in high demand. We can personally vouch for their usefulness and attest to how helpful the Costco staff can be in explaining how to operate them.

WHAT'S IT LIKE TO DO A "SHIFT IN THE LOT"?

Wrangling shopping carts in the Costco parking lot is a challenging but crucial job that most employees have done at some point. In locations like Gilbert, Arizona where the average summer temperature is 107 degrees Fahrenheit, shifts in the parking lot are limited to five hours, hydration is critical, and light-colored shoes and socks are recommended to keep workers cool on the hot tarmac. The electric cart pushers that are used to wrangle and move the carts in the parking lot can handle a maximum of 40 carts at a time, but in parking lots that aren't flat, the number is limited to twenty.

HOW DID ONE COSTCO SHOPPING CART BECOME FAMOUS?

You must be referring to Dash the Legendary Shopping Cart! After the Woodinville, Washington warehouse (#747) replaced the entire fleet of white carts with new gray ones, a single old white cart was recovered from a nearby ravine and reunited with the other carts. In 2019, Dash née Blanco made it to the bigtime: named "employee of the month" and appearing at a parade with the Mayor! Yes, we were lucky enough to find and shop with Dash's help!

WHAT ARE SOME IMPROVEMENTS COSTCO HAS MADE TO ITS SHOPPING CART?

In 2013, Costco unveiled a new and improved shopping cart which was lighter in weight, easier to maneuver, and with lower sides to make it easier to load and unload items. Also, the cart's child seat was higher, wider, and for increased safety, stationary rather than collapsible.

WHAT IS "APPLIED GEOMETRY"?

It's the May 5, 2004 installation by artist Robert Wechsler — then a senior at University of California, Santa Barbara — in the nearby Goleta, California Costco warehouse parking lot. Robert "followed the natural curve" in a line of 236 otherwise ordinary carts to create an artistic "inspiration of the familiar": a cart circle measuring 236 feet in circumference with a 75 feet diameter. Although he got permission from the warehouse manager the night before, the warehouse staff the next morning urged him to complete the project before senior management arrived for an "executive walk."

Illustration of
Robert Wechsler's photograph
of his installation
Applied Geometry, 2004

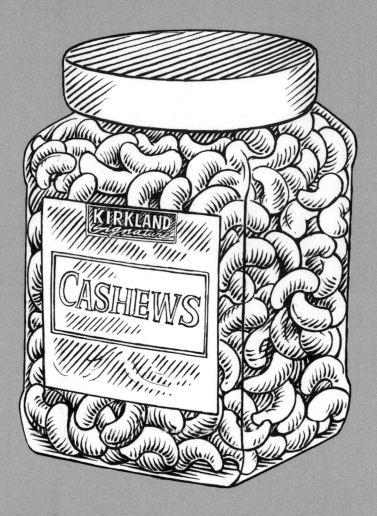

CASHEWS

COSTCO SELLS
HALF OF THE WORLD'S
CASHEWS

WHY ARE THE CONTAINERS SQUARE?

When Costco started selling cashews, they were packaged in round containers. In 2007, Costco's efficiency experts calculated that they could pack more containers of cashews on distribution trucks in square containers. That simple change saved over 400 truckloads of shipping expenses in just the first year, and has saved significantly more as volume has grown. Recently, in an environmentally friendly move, Costco introduced a large, square, refillable, glass container; the cashews to refill the glass containers are now sold in plastic bags.

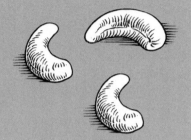

WHAT GRADE OF CASHEWS DOES COSTCO SELL?

Like most nuts, cashews are graded by size, color, condition, and weight. Costco sells only the top grade, which is the largest. The low percentage of unbroken nuts in a container of Costco's whole cashews is impressive, particularly when compared to other retailers, but has little to do with packaging and everything to do with the quality of the nuts. Cashews are lower in protein and fiber than most other nuts, but are an excellent source of phosphorous, magnesium, iron, and other dietary minerals which help maintain bone health.

HOW ARE CASHEWS GROWN AND HARVESTED?

Cashew trees can grow up to 45 feet in height; it takes three years to produce the first fruit and eight years for a full harvest. The fruit is known as a cashew apple, each of which has a single cashew kernel on its bottom. Farmers must wait for the cashew apples to ripen and fall to the ground. They then hand-collect the fallen fruit, use a simple string hand-tool to separate the cashew kernels from the apples, and then spread the kernels out to dry in the shade for a few days. The dried kernels are finally sorted by grade, bagged in jute sacks, and brought to the local village to be weighed and sold before roasting and packaging.

DOES COSTCO RELY ON MORE THAN ONE SOURCE FOR ITS CASHEWS?

Costco works with 2.5 million independent cashew farmers in Africa, ensuring that these small farmers get a fair return and a link to the global market. The average size of an African cashew farm is only about 1.5 acres. Despite the large number of growers, Costco is able to track and trace their sourcing, and also support the farmers with training, construction, AIDS awareness, school kits for children, planting new trees, and investing in processing plants.

WHERE DOES COSTCO PURCHASE CASHEWS?

Most cashews are grown in Africa, India, or Vietnam. For many years, Costco's cashews were purchased in Africa, shelled in Vietnam, and then roasted and packaged in the US. In 2018, Costco partnered with Olam Food Ingredients (OFI), a global leader in sustainable food production, to streamline the process. Cashews are still sourced from Africa and shelled in Vietnam, but roasting and packaging are now also handled in Vietnam rather than in the US. This improvement in the production chain has considerably reduced costs, savings that Costco happily passes along to its members.

IN 2022, COSTCO MEMBERS BOUGHT OVER $300,000 WORTH OF WHOLE CASHEWS EVERY WEEK

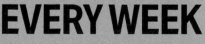

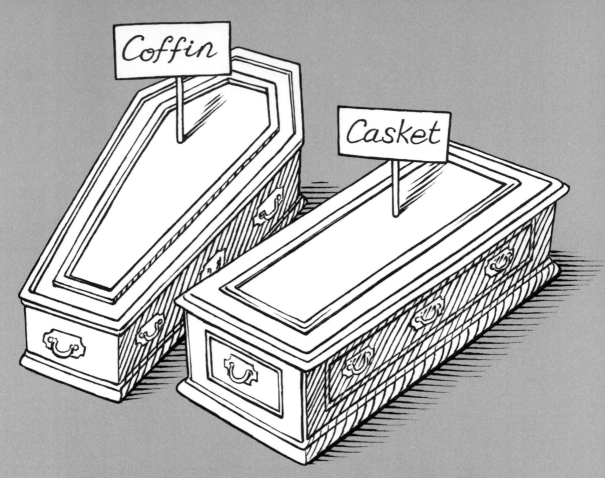

CASKETS & COFFINS

COSTCO EVEN SELLS
CASKETS AND COFFINS
— AT GREAT PRICES

COSTCO SELLS CASKETS AND COFFINS?

Costco offers nine different styles at significantly lower prices than Batesville and Matthews International, the two major manufacturers that account for 82% of the market. A casket at a funeral home may cost as much as $10,000, with the average price about $2,300. Costco's caskets range from $1,149 to $1,499, so the savings are considerable. Originally sourced from a family company in Chicago, the caskets are now made in China for Prime Caskets, a California-based company established by Costco. None of Costco's caskets are entirely wood, so they would not be suitable for religions that prohibit the use of metal in caskets, like Orthodox Judaism.

IS A CASKET THE SAME THING AS A COFFIN?

In most contexts the terms are interchangeable. Technically, a casket is rectangular, a coffin is an elongated hexagon. Costco sells coffins, too, but does not sell urns for cremated remains.

HOW DO I BUY A CASKET OR COFFIN AT COSTCO?

There are kiosk displays at some Costco warehouses, but sales are exclusively online, shipped only to a funeral home, mortuary, or other facility that may hold a casket prior to funeral services. Caskets are generally delivered, shipping included, within three business days. Federal and state laws prohibit funeral homes from adding to the cost of a casket purchased outside a funeral home or refusing to use a casket purchased elsewhere. Unlike those at funeral homes, Costco's caskets are not available for pre-order, which might present a problem for any religions that require burial within 24 hours of death, such as Judaism, although in some cases alternate arrangements can be made for a surcharge.

He actually shouldn't be waiting *on the line* to buy that coffin — they are only available *online!*

CHICKEN

IN THE US, COSTCO SELLS
OVER 100 MILLION ROTISSERIE
CHICKENS EACH YEAR

WHAT'S SPECIAL ABOUT COSTCO'S ROTISSERIE CHICKEN BESIDES THE PRICE?

Tim Rose, a founding officer who was responsible for the introduction of fresh food, decided that each chicken container should have a time stamp to indicate when it came out of the rotisserie. The containers are pulled from the shelf after two hours to ensure the chickens are sold at peak perfection. After that, the meat is "harvested" for other uses, like soup or salad. The chicken is still safe to eat after two hours, but it doesn't taste quite as good. This dedication to quality control is unique to Costco and ensures that your trip to the back of the warehouse is worth it.

HOW MANY ROTISSERIE CHICKENS DOES COSTCO SELL EACH YEAR?

In the US, Costco sells over 100 million chickens each year at $4.99 per bird. Since introduction, the price has not increased, even though production costs have. Costco believes strongly that this unique member value is worth maintaining, instead of increasing the price and capturing as much profit as possible. In this way, it is appropriate that the rotisserie chicken is so iconic for Costco.

WHEN DID COSTCO START SELLING ROTISSERIE CHICKEN?

In 1995, Pierre Riel and Louis Santillo, two Canadian Costco employees, were inspired by Steinberg's, a major Canadian supermarket chain that sold rotisserie chickens. They contacted Henny Penny, an American oven manufacturer, to design a convection oven with a front-facing window so that passersby could watch the chickens being roasted, and bought four-pound chickens from a local farmer. Costco's first rotisserie opened in the Marché Central Costco warehouse, about five miles east of downtown Montréal. When their senior manager returned from vacation the next week, she was somewhat surprised to see the new operation, but they sold over 6,000 chickens the first week. The ovens are now gas-fueled, and the chickens are sold globally.

WHAT WAS "PROJECT RAWHIDE"?

In the 1990s, when rotisserie chicken was first introduced, the average bird was about four pounds. When Costco rolled out the product nationally, the rotisseries were sized for six-pound chickens. Over time, the size of commercial chickens gradually increased until it became difficult for Costco to fit them into the existing rotisseries. In 2015, Costco launched "Project Rawhide" to address the problem by raising and processing their own chickens. In 2019, Costco established Lincoln Premium Poultry, their own vertically integrated poultry farm in Fremont, Nebraska. The 432-acre plant can process two million chickens per week, supplying about one-third of Costco's raw chickens and almost half of its rotisserie chickens. The facility employs about 800 workers, and includes a feed mill, 500 giant barns, and the chicken processing plant. It is estimated to have a $1.2 billion beneficial impact on Nebraska. Costco partners with more than 100 Nebraskan farming families who have shifted from grain crops to chicken farming. The 13,500 tons of feed for the chickens are locally sourced. In overseas locations, chickens are supplied by small local farms.

WHAT STEPS HAS COSTCO TAKEN TO IMPROVE CHICKEN WELFARE?

The 45-day cycle used by Costco is slower than that used by most other major chicken processors. In addition, the top weight for a Costco chicken is significantly below that of the standard commercially raised chicken — a key motivation in manufacturing their own chickens. Costco's chickens spend the majority of their lives at a weight which allows them to stand comfortably. Shifting to slower-growing breeds, as suggested by animal rights activists, could have an adverse environmental impact, including higher lifetime feed demand for the birds, greater energy consumption, and higher waste output, which could raise the chicken program's carbon footprint. Costco is working with its breeders to increase the chickens' leg strength in tandem with their weight gain.

ARE COSTCO'S CHICKENS TREATED HUMANELY?

Famed animal welfare specialist Temple Grandin has advised Costco on its live animal facilities. Even so, Costco was sued by animal rights activists arguing that the 45-day growth cycle places undue strain on chickens, resulting in such fast weight gain that the birds cannot stand on their own legs. Costco has said publicly that it is committed to maintaining "the highest standards of animal welfare, humane processes and ethical conduct throughout the supply chain." As of January 2023, the lawsuit was still pending.

CHINA

Membership Sign-up Area

IN AUGUST 2019, OVER 200,000 NEW MEMBERS — A RECORD NUMBER — SIGNED UP BEFORE THE OPENING OF CHINA'S FIRST COSTCO WAREHOUSE

HOW DID COSTCO BEGIN DOING BUSINESS IN CHINA?

In 2014, after many years of careful consideration, Costco launched a three-stage expansion into China, the world's most populous country with the world's second-largest economy. The first phase was a joint venture with Alibaba's Tmall, China's biggest business-to-consumer online platform, with orders fulfilled by Costco Taiwan, which was already well-established. The second stage was to create a fulfillment center on mainland China. On August 27, 2019, in the third phase, Costco opened its first traditional walk-in Costco warehouse near Hongqino Airport in the Minhang district of Shanghai, China's largest city. On December 8, 2021, a second warehouse opened in Suzhou, followed by a third in Pudong on March 10, 2023.

WERE THE CHINESE COSTCO WAREHOUSES WELL-RECEIVED?

Opening day at the first Costco warehouse on mainland China was tumultuous. Crowds thronged the warehouse, there was a three-hour wait for parking, and traffic backed up for miles. The warehouse closed early, at 2:30 PM — so parents could pick up their children at a nearby daycare center without difficulty. It took several hours for the parking lot and surrounding streets to clear, and the iconic rotisserie chicken was completely sold out when the warehouse closed. The enthusiasm carried over to the openings of the next two warehouses, as well.

IS THERE WIFI IN THE WAREHOUSE?

Nearly 80% of Chinese members pay using a mobile device, so connectivity is essential. On opening day at the first warehouse in Shanghai, not only was the parking lot overflowing, but the broadband in the warehouse was overwhelmed with social media posts; the Wi-Fi and broadband were immediately upgraded to handle the traffic. If you can't visit a Chinese warehouse in person, there are endless YouTube videos available so you can at least visit virtually.

ANYTHING UNIQUE ABOUT THE CHINESE WAREHOUSES?

The fresh food, especially seafood, is different from Costco in many other countries: local seafood includes yellow croaker, pomfret, anchovies, cod, and grouper. You may also find live shellfish like King crab, Maine lobster, Australian black-lipped abalone, fresh baby octopus, or a visually arresting "geoduck," a clam with a six-to-eight inch "foot" sticking out of its shell. Perhaps the most exotic item is dried sea cucumber, a type of sea-slug used frequently in Chinese cuisine. The Sushi department has the same range of large trays found in Costco warehouses in South Korea and Japan, freshly-made and priced very competitively. In the Deli, the rotisserie chicken is sold with its head still attached, which is similar to Taiwan, but different from the rest of the world. The Deli also has German pork knuckles and a variety of prepared food, including shabu-shabu kits and a colorful pork-and-pepper stir-fry. Much of the fresh produce is sourced locally; one Chinese specialty is dragon fruit, an ovoid fruit with a thick red skin and sweet red or white flesh with small crunchy black seeds. Meat is sourced from the US and Australia, but the pork and chicken are locally sourced.

HOW DIFFERENT IS THE FOOD COURT?

The Chinese Food Court is surprisingly similar to a standard US Costco with only a few differences: the hot dogs are 100% pork; pizza is available with seafood toppings; and there's a bulgogi bake in addition to the usual chicken bake. As in South Korea and Taiwan, there are delicious clam chowder and spicy chicken legs. There is also a pork pie, which is about the size of a chicken bake but in a traditional pie format. Perhaps over time the Food Court in China will develop its own unique items — as the Australian ones have done — but for now, if you are expecting to find spareribs or pot stickers, you might be disappointed. The food is excellent, but not especially Chinese.

HOW DID COSTCO COPE WITH COVID IN CHINA?

In the early stages of the Covid pandemic, foot traffic in the Chinese warehouses slowed down as citizens' movements were restricted. In April 2022, Shanghai was entirely locked down and Costco warehouses were closed for several months. However, during the summer the lockdown was gradually lifted. The first day that citizens were no longer restricted, the warehouses were crowded with members eager to return to normalcy — and Costco! As in the US, no Costco employees were laid off during the shutdown.

WHAT'S THE FUTURE OF COSTCO IN CHINA?

Despite the challenges of the pandemic and global shipping constraints, Costco has been unquestionably successful in China. As of March 2023, six additional warehouses were planned in Shanghai, Guangdong, Jiangsu, and Zhejiang provinces.

WHAT IS MOUTAI?

Dating back to the Qing Dynasty (1644-1911), Moutai is China's national liquor, made of distilled fermented sorghum by goverment-owned Kweichow Moutai Company. Known as the "drink of diplomacy," Moutai was famously shared by Premier Zhou Enlai with President Richard M. Nixon during his 1972 visit to China. In 1979, in Washington, DC, Henry Kissinger remarked to Chairman Deng Xiaoping, "I think if we drink enough Moutai we can solve anything." Brewed in the eponymous town, the most popular variety is called Feitan ("flying fairy"). Before the 2019 Mid-Autumn Festival, Costco sold Moutai at the bargain price of ¥1499 (about $210) for a 375-liter bottle resulting in some 10,000 bottles flying off the shelves in only two days. News reports suggest that Kweichow appreciated the opportunity to regain control of the famous liquor's pricing, which speculators had been ramping up beyond the means of most Chinese.

COSTCO

Code of Ethics

Obey the Law
Take care of members
Take care of employees
Respect suppliers
Reward shareholders

COSTCO MIGHT BE ONE OF THE WORLD'S BIGGEST RETAILERS, BUT THEIR CODE OF ETHICS IS A MERE 19 WORDS

CODE OF ETHICS

WHAT IS A CODE OF ETHICS?

It is a set of principles governing behavior. At Costco, it is the foundation of the entire organization, and every employee lives and breathes it every day. Similar to the Golden Rule urging one to do unto others as one would want to be treated, the code of ethics is about decency, respect, and reciprocity.

WHAT IS COSTCO'S MISSION STATEMENT AND CODE OF ETHICS?

Costco's mission is straightforward: to continually provide members with quality goods and services at the lowest possible prices. The code of ethics is only nineteen words, but it is crucial to the company's ongoing success. A sign with the code of ethics is posted near the entry of every warehouse, manufacturing facility, or other building around the world:

> **OBEY THE LAW.**
> **TAKE CARE OF OUR MEMBERS.**
> **TAKE CARE OF OUR EMPLOYEES.**
> **RESPECT OUR SUPPLIERS.**
> **REWARD OUR SHAREHOLDERS.**

WHAT ARE COSTCO'S SUSTAINABILITY PRINCIPLES?

Costco is committed to doing the right thing, not only for its members, employees, suppliers, and shareholders, but also for the communities and environments in which they do business, staying mindful of the company's social and environmental impact. Costco believes it has an obligation and responsibility to do its part in terms of sustainability. These three guiding principles drive Costco's approach in addressing some of the world's most complex problems:

> **"FOR COSTCO TO THRIVE, THE WORLD MUST THRIVE — WE ARE COMMITTED TO DOING OUR PART"**
>
> **"WE FOCUS ON ISSUES RELATED TO OUR BUSINESS AND WHERE WE CAN CONTRIBUTE TO REAL, RESULTS-DRIVEN POSITIVE IMPACT"**
>
> **"WE DO NOT HAVE ALL THE ANSWERS, ARE LEARNING AS WE GO AND SEEK CONTINUOUS IMPROVEMENT"**

WHAT MAKES COSTCO'S CODE OF ETHICS UNIQUE?

Many organizations have a code of ethics, but Costco's is perhaps one of the most concise ever — and one of the few things at Costco that is not super-sized! It dates back to learning that began at FedMart with Sol Price, Jim Sinegal's mentor. During our travels to various Costco warehouses and facilities around the world, we often heard employees quote "Obey the law" in the course of ordinary conversation. It's hard to imagine another company with a code of ethics that is equally omnipresent and important.

COFFEE

COFFEE IS THE WORLD'S
THIRD MOST POPULAR BEVERAGE
AFTER WATER AND TEA

CAN YOU GIVE ME A VERY BRIEF HISTORY OF COFFEE?

Long ago, coffee plants were found growing wild in either Yemen or Ethiopia — depending on who is telling the story — and herders noticed that their goats had difficulty sleeping after eating the plant's bright red fruit (known as "cherries"). Myth has it that monks took advantage of coffee's stimulant properties to stay alert during evening prayers, and nomadic tribes also enjoyed the jolt from a bit of coffee. In the 1400s, people began roasting and grinding the seeds inside the berries (the "beans") and immersing them in boiling water.

WHAT KIND OF COFFEE DOES COSTCO SELL?

Even though coffee usually fills an entire aisle at most Costco warehouses, it is still highly curated. There are a full range of well-known national brands like Folger's, Starbucks, and Dunkin'; regional brands like Peet's and Café Bustelo; and local brands like North Pole Coffee from Alaska. Costco sells coffee in many different forms: instant, whole beans, ground, and individual K-Cup™ pods. There are large grinders near the checkout area at the warehouses for those who want to take home freshly ground coffee.

WHAT IS COSTCO'S POLICY ON FAIR TRADE COFFEE?

All of Costco's Kirkland Signature coffee is Fair Trade certified and audited through the supply chain to meet sustainability and labor standards. The Rogers Company works to ensure that everyone involved in the coffee business benefits from the process. The Rogers Charitable Fund was created to improve the lives of those in areas where coffee is grown.

ARE YOU FINNISH WITH THAT?

America consumes the most coffee overall, but Finland is the largest consumer on a per capita basis. The average Finn drinks almost 4 cups per day. In fact, Finnish law mandates two 10-15 minute coffee breaks every workday!

WHAT IS INVOLVED IN COSTCO'S COFFEE ROASTING PROCESS?

The raw, pale-green coffee beans arrive in huge plastic bags on pallets directly from overseas growers. A master coffee roaster attends the sophisticated computer-controlled roasting process, designed for precision and sustainability; it heats the beans to 450 degrees Fahrenheit before cooling them down and sending them off to be packaged. There is a Quality Assurance area near the roastery for tasting and grading samples based on color and flavor. Controlling the roasting process enables Costco to manage costs and quality to better serve its members. Yes, the aroma in this facility is magnificent!

WHAT CAN YOU TELL ME ABOUT KIRKLAND SIGNATURE COFFEE?

All of Costco's Kirkland Signature coffee is sourced through the Rogers Family Company, based in Lincoln, California, which also manufactures San Francisco Bay Coffee. Kirkland Signature's House Blend is co-branded with Starbucks and is blended and roasted by Starbucks to Costco's specifications; every other variety of Kirkland Signature coffee is roasted at a Costco facility in New Jersey. Costco uses only the milder, more expensive arabica beans, mainly sourced from Brazil, Columbia, and Ethiopia.

KIRKLAND SIGNATURE "ROTATIONAL COLLECTION"
Throughout the year, Costco rotates
four different dark roast Kirkland Signature varieties
sold in three-pound bags of whole beans

SEASON	VARIETY	FLAVOR PROFILE
SPRING	RWANDAN	MEDIUM BODY, JASMINE SCENT, HINTS OF CHOCOLATE AND CITRUS
SUMMER	COSTA RICAN	SWEET AND SMOKY
FALL	GUATEMALAN	WELL-BALANCED, INTENSE, VELVETY FEEL, AND SWEET TANGY FINISH
WINTER	SUMATRAN	SMOOTH, BALANCED, FULL-BODIED

Year-round, Costco also sells
Colombian Supremo (medium roast, slightly sweet, touch of citrus)
and French Roast (dark roast, deep, full-bodied).

COSTCO CONNECTION

THE FOURTH-LARGEST CIRCULATION US PRINT MAGAZINE, SENT TO EVERY COSTCO EXECUTIVE MEMBER MONTHLY

WHAT'S THE CIRCULATION?

Costco Connection has an audited circulation of almost 16 million issues per month. It originally started as a newsprint flyer available in warehouses. In 1997, *Costco Connection* became a full-fledged print magazine, and now has more readers than any other magazine except *Parade* and AARP's two monthly magazines. We estimate that Costco uses five million pounds of recycled paper each month to print the magazine, which is sent by US mail, and is also available at warehouses and online.

DOES *COSTCO CONNECTION* INCLUDE ADVERTISING?

National brands as well as smaller vendors compete for advertising space in the magazine to reach a demographic that averages 54-years-old with a median income of $119,000. In early 2023, a full-color, full-page ad cost about $200,000. Costco will sometimes share the cost with a vendor in an arrangement called "co-op" advertising. Costco strives to keep costs down (e.g., paper, printing, postage, and handling) and then offsets much of the cost with advertising revenue.

WHAT'S INSIDE *COSTCO CONNECTION?*

The magazine includes a cover story; special seasonal sections contributed by Costco buyers like "For Your Home/Table/Entertainment/Health"; "Inside Costco," featuring member services in "Looking Out for You"; exciting new items in "Treasure Hunt"; and "Recipes". There are also regular monthly columns by respected columnists, like Suze Orman on finance and Peter Greenberg on travel, who will answer members' questions in their articles.

ARE THERE OTHER FEATURES OF INTEREST?

Every month there's an interesting note from the publisher along with member comments. For many years before her retirement, Pennie Clark Ianniciello, Costco's longtime head book buyer, wrote a popular monthly column called "Pennie's Picks." (Full disclosure: Pennie worked as a consultant on this book.) Book and media suggestions from the current buying team are included in "For Your Entertainment." As with Costco's merchandise, the magazine's content is varied and intended to help members by promoting products and services that are available either in warehouse, online, or both.

ANY EXAMPLES OF A TYPICAL COVER STORY?

The cover is timely and targets the broad readership. The July 2022 cover story, "Queens of the Grill," profiled five women in the competitive BBQ world, along with their recipes and bios. Christmas 2021 featured a profile of Sir Paul McCartney to coincide with the holiday release of his book "The Lyrics," which was sold at Costco. The August 2022 cover story was one of our favorites: "Crazy for Costco," celebrating the myriad fans of Costco!

COSTCO SERVICES

IN 2021, COSTCO'S AUTO PROGRAM SOLD MORE THAN 800,000 VEHICLES — TRIPLE THE NUMBER SOLD IN 2011 — WITHOUT ANY HAGGLING

WHAT ARE COSTCO SERVICES?

In 1997, Costco created an Executive Membership level and began offering a range of high-quality, competitively priced services to distinguish the new level from basic Gold Star membership. Over time, these services, which are available on websites in the US, UK, and Canada — in partnership with third-party providers — became available to all members (although Executive members get additional savings). The idea was to provide services that members could trust would be fairly priced and reliable, without the hassle of negotiating with vendors. The pre-existing Auto Program was immediately folded into Costco Services, and others were added bit by bit. As of January 2023, Costco offers 23 different services to its members, ranging from auto sales to life insurance, from check printing to vacation packages, and even identity theft protection. [SEE "MEMBERS"]

ARE THE HVAC, KITCHEN FITTINGS, AND WATER DELIVERY KIOSKS NEAR THE WAREHOUSE EXIT ALSO PART OF COSTCO SERVICES?

Yes, Costco has contracted with third-party vendors and negotiated set low prices for Costco members for these services. For example, Lennox Heating and Air Conditioning, one of the leading manufacturers of HVAC systems, handles HVAC equipment installation.

WHAT KIND OF INSURANCE IS AVAILABLE AT COSTCO?

Costco contracts with third-party providers of auto insurance, so after you've bought your car through the Auto Program you can also get accident or theft coverage. Costco Services' insurance portfolio extends to home insurance, life insurance, small business health and vision insurance, and pet insurance. The third-party providers Costco partners with are nationally recognized top-quality vendors like Connect/American Family for auto and home insurance.

I CAN BUY A CAR FROM AN AUTO DEALER AT A PRE-ARRANGED, SET PRICE?

In the early 1990s, working with selected dealerships across the country, Costco launched the Auto Program to sell a curated selection of vehicles for pre-arranged prices. Members appreciate being able to pay the price they see online without haggling, and can also save up to 15% on parts and services at many of these dealerships.

COSTCO ALSO HELPS WITH CAR RENTALS AND OTHER TRAVEL SERVICES?

In 2000, at the instigation of Costco founding officer Court Newberry, Costco purchased Pacific Escapes Travel Agency and began offering high-value travel services for very low prices. The following year, travel was integrated into Costco.com. In 2009, cruises were added and, two years later, the Low Price Finder car rental app, which works with major car rental companies to bring low rates to Costco members, joined the growing portfolio of travel services. Costco Travel has since grown into a significant business, employing 900 travel agents in the US and Canada, and offering a variety of travel plans. During the pandemic, Costco Travel did not lay off any of its employees even though travel dropped precipitously. The business has since rebounded and continues to grow.

COSTCO WHOLESALE INDUSTRIES

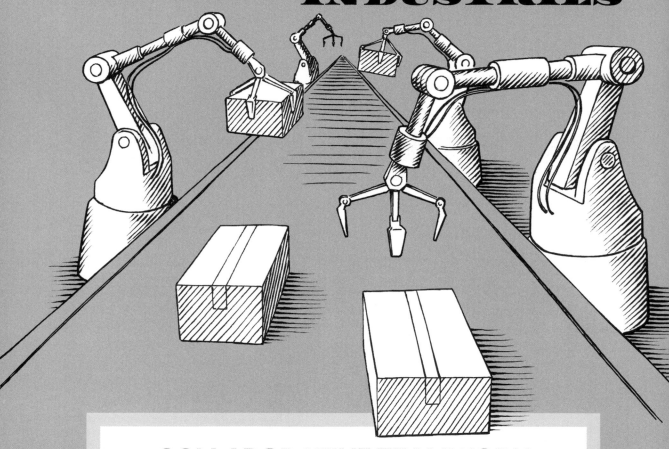

COLLABORATIVE TEAMWORK AND LEAN SIX SIGMA MANUFACTURING ARE THE SECRETS TO CWI'S SUCCESS

WHAT IS "COSTCO WHOLESALE INDUSTRIES"?

Costco Wholesale Industries (CWI) — a separate division of Costco Wholesale — operates manufacturing businesses (including special packaging, optical labs, meat processing, and coffee roasting) at locations around the world. The range of products is extraordinary, from prescription eyeglasses to hot dogs and ground beef. **[SEE "OPTICAL," "MEAT," AND "HOT DOGS"]** The common theme is reducing manufacturing costs to increase value for Costco members; CWI is a large part of the reason that Costco is able to offer such competitive pricing. For example, by bringing hot dog production in-house to CWI, Costco was able to maintain the pricing of the $1.50 hot-dog-and-soda combination at the Food Court.

WHAT KIND OF FOOD PACKAGING DOES CWI HANDLE?

Most Kirkland Signature nuts are packaged and shipped from these facilities, where they arrive in bulk quantities and get repackaged for sale in the warehouses. One Halloween favorite unique to CWI is a candy bar variety bag with treats from three different major candy manufacturers in one bag. Costco negotiated a deal with Hershey, Mars, and Nestlé in which these arch-rivals allowed Costco to combine their products into one special bag for members.

DOES COSTCO REALLY ROAST AND PACKAGE COFFEE?

Costco operates a state-of-the-art coffee roasting and packing facility as part of CWI. The facility in New Jersey handles all of the Kirkland Signature coffee that is not co-branded and roasted in partnership with Starbucks. Beans from around the world are shipped to the CWI facility, graded for taste and quality, roasted and packed, whole or ground, into Kirkland Signature bags for warehouses worldwide. **[SEE "COFFEE"]**

HOW DOES COSTCO MAINTAIN QUALITY AND SAFETY AT THESE FACILITIES?

Quality assurance teams inspect incoming items before repacking. Inspection of nuts and other food products is especially important, given safety and hygiene concerns, and if these items are not up to the specifications in Costco's purchase order, they are returned to the vendor. In the packing process there are further safeguards at each step to ensure that packages are packed safely and at the proper weight. Equipment is cleaned regularly, at the beginning and end of each shift. Safety is a top priority: at the meat processing facilities, meat is checked often throughout processing to ensure that it is safe. Costco takes justifiable pride in maintaining quality standards that are more rigorous than those required by the federal government.

WHAT IS LEAN SIX SIGMA MANUFACTURING?

CWI combines the Six Sigma Initiative pioneered in the 1980s by Motorola and Toyota's Lean Manufacturing, based on the Japanese *kaizen* approach of continuous improvement. Six Sigma improves processes by reducing variables such as safety, production, and shrinkage. Simply put: remove variables, increase efficiency. An example of this at CWI is the painted yellow outline on the floor to indicate the specific location for a garbage can, rather than having to search for one, unsure of where it might be. Having equipment in the correct place also means that employees are where they need to be, too. The Lean System encourages collaborative teamwork to improve performance by systematically removing waste and reducing variation, gathering input and suggestions from employees to improve processes. For example, if you ever notice a cashier at a Costco warehouse moving your cart to the very end of the register belt to pack your purchase, know that this was suggested by a Costco employee!

WHAT KIND OF NON-FOOD ITEMS ARE PACKAGED AT CWI?

The sophisticated technology at these CWI plants produces customized thermoplastic packages for various non-food and specialty items. For example, special gift packages of Olay Regenerist face cream and the co-branded Kirkland Signature Borghese skin care line are both packed in specially designed plastic bubble units unique to Costco. Recently, in an effort to address sustainability issues associated with plastic, Costco has redesigned this kind of packaging to cut the amount of plastic by 50%. [SEE "SUSTAINABILITY"]

ALL SCRAPS OF PLASTIC TRIMMED FROM PACKAGING MOLDS AND UP TO 850 POUNDS OF SHRINK WRAP ARE RECYCLED EVERY DAY AT A CWI FACILITY

HOW MUCH OF THE MANUFACTURING IS AUTOMATED?

The facilities use state-of-the-art automation, but also employ about 300 people at each location to supervise and do the kind of hand-packing that industrial robots cannot. For example, robots work on an assembly line to place bags of Kirkland Signature Trail Mix into boxes for shipping to warehouses — and stack these boxes onto pallets — while employees still hand-pack Nabisco Variety Pack boxes with five different snack crackers and cookies. The robots are pretty cool to watch, but rarely do they make Lean System suggestions.

EVERY LITTLE BIT OF SAVINGS HELPS REDUCE COSTS AND INCREASE VALUE FOR COSTCO MEMBERS

CREDIT CARDS

IN 1999,
COSTCO BEGAN ACCEPTING
CREDIT CARDS

WHY DID COSTCO BEGIN ACCEPTING CREDIT CARDS?

From Costco's opening, in 1983, credit cards were not accepted. By the 1990s, however, credit cards were becoming common-place as new electronic devices remedied delays at checkout, making these transactions the fastest way to process sales. In August 1999, after Costco's initial foray with the Discover card, American Express approached Costco with a unique business proposition: a co-branded card for all Costco members included as a perk of membership. The new partnership expanded Costco's reach, and credit card spending and member retention improved. Amex's business model enabled Costco to deliver a great value to its members.

DID FEDMART, COSTCO'S PREDECESSOR, HAVE ANY PROBLEMS BECAUSE THEY DIDN'T ACCEPT CREDIT CARDS?

Sol was never a fan of charge cards, famously saying "It's against my religion for customers to go into debt to shop," so FedMart accepted only cash and checks, which were collected in black plastic garbage bags and stored overnight for deposit the next morning. One evening, a well-informed thief stole all of the bags. Ever pragmatic, Sol switched to see-through bags so future robbers would hopefully take only the cash and leave the less-easily negotiated checks.

THE AMERICAN EXPRESS/COSTCO CARD WAS SO POPULAR — WHAT HAPPENED?

In 2014, toward the end of a five-year contract, Costco asked Amex, which was well-known to charge more than other vendors, to reduce its transaction fees. Amex CEO Ken Chenault declined, and Costco opened the contract for credit card services to other bidders. Citibank's 0.2-0.3% transaction fee was about half of what Amex was charging and offered another increase in reach; at the end of 2016, Citibank had 335 million credit cards in circulation, dwarfing Amex's 47.5 million. The Costco/Amex breakup was announced in February 2015; and by June 2016, the new Costco Anywhere Visa card by Citi was launched — with additional member benefits.

HOW DID THE BREAKUP WITH COSTCO IMPACT AMERICAN EXPRESS?

Costco members reportedly represented 10% of Amex card-holders and 20% of the spending on the card. After the split with Costco, American Express stock declined briefly, falling close to 6% on the day of the announcement. However, Amex was able to replace the lost volume within two years. The stock price recovered in that two year period, and surpassed where it had been before the announcement of the break.

DELI

ROTISSERIE CHICKEN IS
ONLY ONE OF THE COSTCO DELI
SECTION'S TASTY DELIGHTS!

WHY IS THE DELI SECTION AT THE BACK OF THE WAREHOUSE?

The Deli is usually adjacent to Meat and Fish because they share key ingredients and refrigeration. The Deli has Kirkland Signature dishes freshly prepared on premises, but also includes packaged foods that require refrigeration — like cheese, hummus, sausages, and smoked fish — which are displayed in taller coolers adjacent to the freshly prepared food. Costco's freshly made sushi and other fish dishes are also in this section. **[SEE "JAPAN"]**

HOW MANY ITEMS ARE TYPICALLY IN THE FRESHLY PREPARED DELI SECTION?

The top-selling rotisserie chicken is situated in the center of the tasty Deli landscape, surrounded by as many as 25 different freshly made offerings. The menu varies around the world, but common items might include chicken Caesar salad, shepherd's pie, "Hye roller" wraps or other sandwiches, shrimp salad, quesadilla or taco kits, macaroni and cheese, and stuffed peppers, to name a few. There are also national and seasonal specialties: Mexican Delis offer paella and pacaña on weekends, and we fondly recall the Spanish Deli's *pastel salado* ("salted cake"), a layered serving of bread, seafood salad, and cream cheese topped with smoked salmon.

D

ARE THERE "WOW" ITEMS IN THE DELI?

Madrid's Deli is famous for its large displays of Iberico ham legs. In Seoul, we wondered how long it would take to consume one of the 44-pound Zanetti Provolone Mandarones hanging in a refrigerated end aisle case. ("Mandarones" because of their resemblance to giant mandarin oranges.) This large, wax-covered, string-tied piece of cheese is considered the ideal method for aging cheese without moisture loss. Some seafood "wow" items that have dazzled us would surely include caviar in Stockholm and the freshly made sushi and sashimi in Asia. **[SEE "JAPAN," "SOUTH KOREA," "SPAIN," AND "SWEDEN"]**

ANY TASTY PRE-PACKAGED DESSERT ITEMS IN THE DELI SECTION?

Deli sections offer a stunning array of pre-packaged desserts including macarons, mousse in many flavors, panna cotta, Belgian chocolate souffle cakes, and more. These items are usually sold in multi-packs of individual servings, but you might also find an entire Junior's Cheesecake or Carrot Cake in Deli.

IS EVERYTHING IN DELI READY TO SERVE?

Some Deli items, like ravioli lasagna or meatloaf, are pre-cooked and only need to be reheated, while others like bulgogi beef are raw and require cooking. Detailed instructions are printed on the labels. At Thanksgiving, Costco sells a ready-to-serve family dinner that only needs to be reheated: a large roasted turkey breast, mashed potatoes, and green beans. You might find irresistible St. Louis ribs next to the rotisserie chicken, both of which are fully cooked.

WHO INVENTS THE RECIPES FOR THE FRESHLY PREPARED KIRKLAND SIGNATURE ITEMS?

The Costco Test Kitchen at the Issaquah Home Office has seven professional chefs who test-drive ideas for the Deli, Bakery, and Food Court submitted by employees and members alike; the chefs determine which recipes work best. Chicken street tacos, for example, were invented to use the preponderance of chicken thighs from harvested rotisserie chickens (the white meat was easier to redeploy). The team considered a wrap and a salad before creating the popular taco kit. In fact, the taco kit's lime cilantro dressing was such a hit that Costco now sells it as a stand-alone product!

WHAT IS STOCKED IN THE TALL COOLERS?

The tall coolers in the Deli offer a culinary Treasure Hunt, varying considerably by location and region. In Honolulu, you might find pineapple sausage, whereas in Anchorage the sausage could be reindeer. In Asia, the exotic Deli items are too numerous to list: in Hiroshima, we enjoyed chilled octopus shreds in wasabi sauce and a pre-packaged salad of small, dried sardines with walnuts. The cheese buyers source globally. Product from cheese suppliers who can handle Costco's volume demand might be considered for Kirkland Signature branding, while smaller, artisanal products are scheduled on rotation to add variety. Regional buying teams are responsible for cured meats, hummus, pesto, and the other locally sourced tall cooler items.

WHAT ARE SOME KIRKLAND SIGNATURE HIGHLIGHTS FROM THE DELI?

Two of our favorite Kirkland Signature items are located in the Deli: KS Pesto, which is made with Genovese basil, and KS Smoked Salmon. Happily, both can be found in most Costco Deli sections around the world. The KS cheese selection ranges from goat cheese logs to large wheels of brie and square plastic containers of grated aged parmigiano. Rest assured, there are a myriad of KS Deli items — most of which we have dutifully sampled in our travels!

ROTISSERIE CHICKENS

are only sold for two hours after they come out of the oven. After that, the meat is "harvested" and used for other delicious items, ranging from salad to wraps to soup. Sometimes you will find vacuum-packed bags of harvested rotisserie chicken breast in the Deli, ready to take home and use in your own recipe.

E-COMMERCE

COSTCO'S E-COMMERCE
BUSINESS HAS BEEN PROFITABLE
SINCE DAY ONE

WHEN DID COSTCO BEGIN SELLING ONLINE?

Relatively late in the game — 1998 — Costco began selling online via Costco.com. Sales the next year were $8.5 million. By August 2018, even though less than half of Costco's members were shopping online, the business had already grown to $6 *billion* in sales. Costco's e-commerce objective is to generate sales incremental to walk-in warehouses, replicating rather than replacing the in-person experience. In 2022, Costco's US online sales amounted to $14.3 billion, 6.4% of total sales — more than double what it was in 2018. Costco.com is available in eight countries: US, Canada, Mexico, the UK, Korea, Taiwan, Japan, and Australia, and there are plans to expand further. Costco co-founder Jim Sinegal rightfully considers the online launch one of the company's ten watershed moments.

WHAT WERE THE CHALLENGES OF SETTING UP COSTCO.COM?

The information systems team had to develop an intuitive platform that was easy to navigate and reliable. It also had to take into account sales tax in different states and tax systems in other countries. Costco.com stocks more than twice as many SKUs as the typical physical warehouse — about 10,000 vs. the typical 3,800 — carrying many big and bulky items like large appliances or furniture, or selling seasonal holiday items for a longer period of time than in the warehouse. Savvy members know that there are items in the warehouse that are not sold online (and vice versa), which helps minimize cannibalization of sales between the two platforms.

COURT NEWBERRY

While working part-time at FedMart during high school, Court met Jim Sinegal who later hired him as Costco's 13th employee and a founding officer. Court managed Costco's third warehouse, in Spokane, Washington, and opened the Kirkland, Washington warehouse. Later, he set up the Bay Area regional office and helped open the first warehouse in Richmond, California. In 1993, Court moved to the Home Office to replace retiring Food & Sundries Buyer Stan McMurry.

Court built the Costco Services business, including starting the Travel business. In 2009, he moved to Costco's e-commerce platform, which he ran until his retirement in 2015.

ARE THERE SEPARATE DEPOTS FOR E-COMMERCE?

Costco.com has two depots dedicated to e-commerce: in Frederick, Maryland and in Mira Loma, California, both co-located with standard depots. The Mira Loma depot, almost 500,000 square feet, is about twice the size of the one in Maryland. In just two weeks during the 2018 holiday rush, the Mira Loma depot printed and processed 2.3 *million* paper "pick tickets" for workers to fulfill online orders. If stacked in a pile, those tickets would be taller than the Empire State Building. Since then, Costco has gone paperless, relying on customizable electronic assistants to direct the picking process.

ANY "WOW" E-COMMERCE ITEMS?

Yes, of course! There are often "wow" jewelry items for warehouse grand openings to help generate excitement, but Costco.com carries these items more consistently. Costco has a reputation for bulk-selling, but a 72-pound wheel of aged Parmigiano Reggiano cheese might be too large even for a regular Costco warehouse; however, this is the kind of item you can find at Costco.com. In 2007, Costco.com even sold a Cobra sports car. We can't tell you the price.

IN 2016, COSTCO SOLD OVER 4 BILLION EGGS — 11 MILLION EVERY DAY!

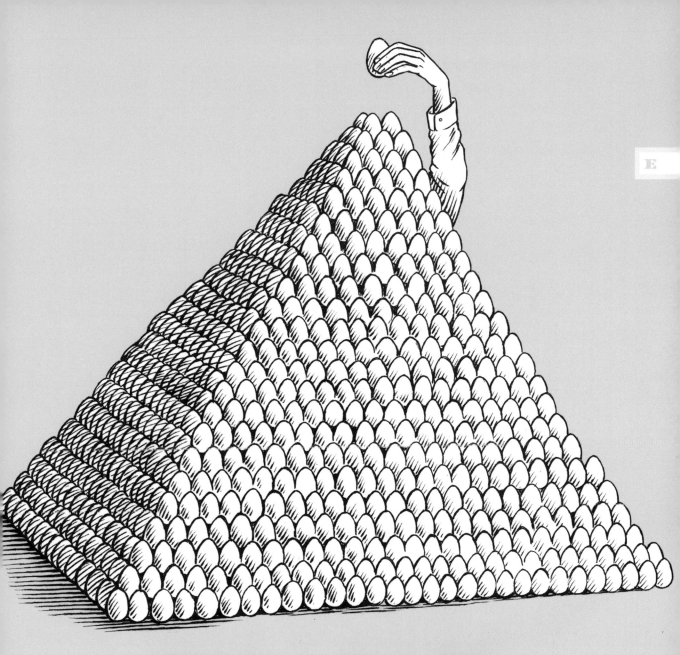

EGGS

WHAT KINDS OF CHICKEN EGGS DOES COSTCO SELL?

Costco sells two kinds of chicken eggs: Large Grade AA cage-free and Organic Large Grade A free-range. The former are laid by hens that live cage-free in barns where they are fed, but are free to venture outside. The latter are from pasture-based hens that forage for their own food, can roost in portable shelters at night or in bad weather, but otherwise roam freely.

WHAT OTHER KINDS OF EGGS DOES COSTCO SELL?

In France you may find duck eggs; in Canada, quail eggs; and in the UK, light-blue chicken eggs. Costco also sells refrigerated containers of Kirkland Signature egg whites. Since spring 2022, Costco has been selling JUST Egg — a plant-based, environmentally friendly egg-substitute made entirely from mung beans — produced by Eat JUST, a San Francisco-based "alt-protein" company.

WHAT'S THE DIFFERENCE BETWEEN GRADE AA AND GRADE A?

The difference between these two grades has nothing to do with the size of the egg and everything to do with the characteristics of the egg whites: Grade AA whites are thicker and firmer than those of Grade A eggs.

HOW DOES COSTCO SOURCE SUCH LARGE QUANTITIES OF EGGS?

Costco's eggs come from local family farms around the world, many of which have been working with Costco for years. For example, in Hawaii Costco works with Oahu-based Waialua Farm to provide local eggs to Hawaiian warehouses. In 2005, Costco began the move to cage-free production, but the process is taking time. Otherwise, Costco would have deprived other retailers of product and driven prices sky-high. In 2015, animal rights activists protested that only 20% of Costco's eggs had been changed to cage-free sourcing. Ryan Gosling, Brad Pitt, and Bill Maher publicly scolded the company; activists sponsored billboards in New York's Times Square criticizing Costco's perceived lack of progress. Costco has since accelerated the transition.

IS COSTCO COMMITTED TO CAGE-FREE EGG PRODUCTION AROUND THE WORLD?

Costco was the first US retailer to make that commitment on a world-wide basis. Costco's egg production in the US was *mostly* cage-free by 2021, with Mexico, Iceland, France, and Spain already 100% cage-free. In other countries the percentage was lower, reflecting the limited availability of cage-free egg production facilities, particularly in Asia. Costco has made progress in Taiwan: increasing from 0% in 2019 to 8.1% in 2021. In December 2020, Costco announced plans to build a cage-free 50,000-hen facility in China to provide cage-free eggs for its growing China business.

EMERGENCIES

IN AN EMERGENCY,
COSTCO DISTRIBUTES
FREE BASIC SUPPLIES
TO ANYONE IN NEED

HOW DOES COSTCO COPE WITH EMERGENCIES?

The thirty-person Home Office risk-management team attempts to plan for every possible business disruption and shares this information on the company intranet. Costco's logistics department carefully manages inventory of essentials like water, bath tissue, first aid supplies, rice, pasta, and other basics. During the early days of the pandemic, Costco employees stepped up to work extra shifts at warehouses and throughout the distribution system. Unlike many other businesses, Costco stayed the course without any layoffs during the pandemic — yet another reason for Costco's extremely low employee turnover rate. The Costco President's Award is given to employees for many extraordinary contributions, including saving a life on the job. **[SEE "EMPLOYEES"]**

WHAT ABOUT EARTHQUAKE-PRONE REGIONS LIKE JAPAN?

Costco warehouses in Japan are designed and constructed to withstand earthquakes. While they have sustained some damage during severe earthquakes, the damage has generally been contained. One unfortunate exception was the collapse of a parking ramp during an earthquake at the Machida, Japan warehouse, which led to two deaths outside the warehouse. All new Japanese warehouses are built with fire shutters — steel barriers — that drop down during a fire to seal off and isolate different sections of the warehouse floor and limit any fire damage, but also constrain pallet placement. Japanese Costco warehouses have earthquake drills every three months which involve employees as well as members. **[SEE "JAPAN"]**

COVID-19

During the early stage of
the pandemic, Costco paid
staff aged 65 or older (or with
underlying health conditions)
to stay home on full pay,
and paid time-and-a-half
to those who were
able to work.

HOW DOES COSTCO DEAL WITH SITUATIONS IN WHICH THE WAREHOUSE BUILDING MAY BE IN DANGER?

Costco warehouses typically close before a potentially dangerous storm hits, to ensure the safety of employees and members. The warehouses and depots are well-built, and few suffer structural damage, although in 2015 an Australian depot was destroyed by a particularly strong hailstorm. The building had to be razed, so Costco rented facilities nearby while the new one was built. In August 2017 Hurricane Harvey caused massive flood damage to the Hubble, Texas Costco warehouse. The extensive repairs and renovation were completed within only 96 days.

EMPLOYEES

AFTER THE FIRST YEAR OF EMPLOYMENT, COSTCO'S EMPLOYEE TURNOVER RATE IS A MERE 7-9% ANNUALLY

WHAT IS THE PATH TO PROMOTION?

Most employees start out in the Food Court or wrangling shopping carts in the parking lot. Costco hires laterally in a few departments with specific technical expertise — for example, butchers or pharmacists — but current employees can also qualify for these positions. Managers are expected to spend 90% of their time *teaching* employees, following Sol Price's philosophy that animals are trained, but people are taught. New warehouses open frequently and are staffed by local hires as well as relocated employees. Unlike most large companies, employees are reviewed annually on the anniversary of their original employment — rather than all at the same time. A key focus at all levels is "readiness for promotion."

HOW DOES COSTCO TREAT PART-TIME EMPLOYEES?

Although warehouses never have more than 50% of employees working less than 24 hours per week, those part-time employees are an important part of Costco's workforce. After three months on the job, part-time employees qualify for excellent benefits including paid time off, health and life insurance, and a 401(k) plan with 50% company match. In the US, part-time employees are also eligible for Costco's Employee Scholarship program.

Everyone at Costco — even top management—
wears a name badge.
Here's a badge color decoder:

BADGE COLOR	YEARS OF SERVICE
WHITE	1–25 YEARS
SILVER	25–40 YEARS
GOLD	40+ YEARS

CAN YOU TELL ME ABOUT COSTCO'S WORKFORCE?

As of September 2022, Costco had about 304,000 employees worldwide, almost 70% in the US. Employee productivity — total revenues divided by the number of employees — was a staggering $747,000 per employee, more than twice the level of other comparable retailers. Over one-third of Costco's employees have ten years or more service with the company, and about 12,000 employees have at least 25 years of service.

WHY ARE EMPLOYEES SO WELL-COMPENSATED?

It's not altruism, it's good business — and it minimizes disruption, maximizes productivity and loyalty, and is a significant competitive advantage. Non-salaried employees earn over three times more than the 2023 US minimum wage of $7.25 per hour. They also get regularly scheduled annual increases and bonus checks based on hours worked, and a free turkey every Thanksgiving. In February 2021, when CEO Craig Jelinek testified about compensation before the US Senate, Costco's average hourly wage for non-salaried US employees was about $24 per hour, before overtime. Senior managers, who are salaried, can be paid well into six figures.

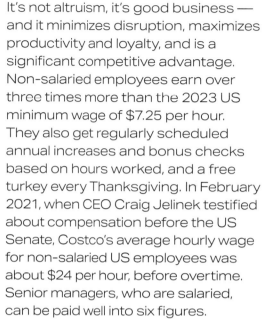

DO THE EMPLOYEES WHO GIVE OUT SAMPLES WORK FOR COSTCO?

The workers who spread joy by dispensing samples work for Club Demonstration Services (CDS), Costco's exclusive in-house marketing provider. As of 2019, CDS had 31,000 associates who handle in-store sampling, demonstrations, and road shows in ten countries/regions, manage over three million events each year, and engage almost three *billion* consumers. CDS employees receive generous benefits and salary, but are not Costco employees. During Covid, when in-store sampling was discontinued for a period of time, many of them were hired by Costco.

HOW WERE EMPLOYEES TREATED DURING COVID?

Employees with underlying health risks, or those over 65, received full pay to stay home at the beginning of the pandemic, when they were at greater risk. Employees who came to work received supplemental pay. No one was laid off. One employee told of a colleague who had recently passed away from Covid; the warehouse general manager personally reached out to each warehouse employee to let them know the sad news. That manager's actions reflected the common feeling that employees are more than just colleagues — they are family.

HOW IS OUTSTANDING EMPLOYEE SERVICE RECOGNIZED?

A select few employees who have literally saved a life while on the job — or made another comparable contribution — receive the President's Award, which is presented by the CEO with a gold badge and cash reward. In the past decade, some 200 employees have received this prestigious honor. The monthly employee magazine has two columns celebrating outstanding performance: "Above & Beyond" for those praised by Costco members and "Badge to Badge" with compliments from fellow employees.

DOES COSTCO HAVE UNIONS?

Prior to the merger with Costco, many Price Club warehouses were unionized, and remain so. Jim Sinegal and Dick DiCerchio invited the Teamsters to unionize the first Costco warehouse, but given the salaries and benefits Costco was offering, there was no apparent reason for unionization. One warehouse in Canada unionized and then later rescinded it. The fact that less than 10% of Costco locations are unionized speaks to the superior employee work conditions.

SAFETY FIRST

31 : 23 : 42 : 509

DAYS · HOURS · MINUTES · SECONDS

#462 CARLSBAD
SAFETY BEGINS WITH YOU!

COSTCO
WHOLESALE

F

FISH

IN 2014, COSTCO'S FISH SALES TOPPED $1.5 BILLION

WHAT KINDS OF FISH DOES COSTCO SELL?

The top-selling fish at Costco are salmon, shrimp, and tilapia, but they are just part of the vast array of fresh and frozen seafood varieties sold at warehouses around the world. A few examples: wild swordfish in NYC, blanched whole octopus and live lobsters in Seoul, fresh sushi in Japan, and fresh king prawns in Stockholm. Costco's fresh fish is globally high in quality and low in price.

DOES COSTCO WORRY ABOUT SUSTAINABILITY?

Absolutely. Costco takes a number of steps to ensure their gargantuan fish program is sustainable, not selling endangered wild fish. Much of Costco's fish is farmed, but the wild fish is responsibly sourced, with a Marine Stewardship Council certification. Costco also participates in Fishery Improvement Projects — multi-stakeholder projects to improve the sustainability of seafood sourcing — in numerous countries, including Belize, Brazil, Costa Rica, Ecuador, Honduras, Morocco, Nicaragua, Peru, the Philippines, Sri Lanka, Suriname, and Taiwan.

DICK DiCERCHIO

On June 5, 2010, Dick DiCerchio, one of Costco's Founding Officers, retired leaving behind a "legacy of innovation and leadership that will not be forgotten." Dick began as a box boy at FedMart, where he first met Jim Sinegal in the 1960s. In 1983, Jeff Brotman and Jim hired Dick as VP, Operations before the first Costco warehouse opened.

For almost twenty years, Dick ran Costco's Merchandising, Membership, and Marketing departments and then was the first Chief Diversity Officer. While at Costco, Dick also ran depot operations, construction and facilities operations, and ancillary businesses.

Dick was on the Costco Board of Directors for 25 years.

HOW BIG IS COSTCO'S SALMON BUSINESS?

In 2015, Costco was selling 600,000 pounds of salmon *per week*, and shifted much of their sourcing from Chile to Norway because the Scandinavian sources could supply high-quality salmon at lower prices. This change impacted not only the pricing of Chilean salmon, which dropped by 10 cents per pound, but also the balance of trade in *both* countries.

WHAT IS "THE SALMON STORY"?

In 1987, Costco began to sell fresh meat and fish. At first, they sold fresh whole salmon for $5.99 per pound. Over time, the team improved quality by removing the skin, the fins, and bones, while *lowering* the price even though the process became more labor-intensive. As sales increased, they began buying in huge volume from Chile and Canada and were able to reduce the price even further, to $4.79 per pound. The price has increased over the decades, but this story remains unchanged.

WHY IS "THE SALMON STORY" SO IMPORTANT TO COSTCO'S CULTURE?

Dick DiCerchio was the first to tell this story to new employees as an example of corporate culture — and the story is being told to this day. It's prominently displayed in the main lobby at the Home Office in Issaquah, Washington, and in regional offices around the world. Counterintuitively, as the product became more time-consuming and expensive to produce, the price dropped, quality improved, and sales increased. As Jim Sinegal says simply: "That's what we do."

F

3,99

1/4 POUND *PLUS*
ALL BEEF HOT DOG
AND 22 oz. SODA (With Refill)
£**1.50**

CHIC
BAK
1 FZA

FOOD COURT

IN 2022,
COSTCO FOOD COURT
SALES TOTALED
$1.4 BILLION

75

CHICKEN NUGGET & POTATO
チキンナゲット&ポテト
¥880

SUNDAE
DE VAINILLA 1,69

F

Peytingur
450 kr.

WHAT IS THE HISTORY OF COSTCO'S FOOD COURT?

Around 1984, Costco and Price Club both began selling hot dogs. [SEE "HOT DOGS"] At one point, Costco's Food Court was called Café 150, in honor of the iconic $1.50 hot dog-and-soda combo; Price Club's snack bar was called the Pizza Kitchen, although hot dogs were also sold. After the Costco/Price Club merger in 1994, the Food Court was born. In 2018, Costco Food Courts sold 377 million items in 164 million separate transactions, for a weekly average of $36,000 per location.

WHAT IS AN EXAMPLE OF A FOOD COURT "SAVE STORY"?

Costco employees are always on the lookout for ways to save money, known as a "save story." One of the best examples was bringing hot dog manufacturing in-house, which enabled Costco to maintain the $1.50 pricing on the hot dog/soda combo. **[SEE "HOT DOGS"]** Another example was the switch to concentrated pizza sauce, which saved $2.2 million per year in shipping costs (9.3 million fewer pounds to ship). In an operation that uses 1.6 million pounds of ketchup per year, seemingly small changes can mean big savings — like a change to a higher quality, larger, "Texas" hot dog roll, which saves $95,000 per year.

WHAT ARE THE KIOSKS AT THE FOOD COURT?

In 2018, Costco tested point-of-sales kiosks at four Food Court locations: Covington, Washington; Tucson, Arizona; and Pacoima and Tustin, California. Members select and pay for food at the kiosk, then wait in line to pick up, which speeds customer throughput considerably. The technology was an immediate success, bumping Food Court sales by as much as 10% overnight. Kiosks are now in use throughout most of the US and overseas.

WHAT'S A TYPICAL WORKDAY LIKE AT THE FOOD COURT?

At 6 AM, the first two employees arrive, print production logs, and begin the day's prep by restocking pizza boxes and other materials. At 8 AM, a third employee joins them and the prep continues: folding pizza boxes, and prepping pizza dough and chicken bakes. Warehouse doors open for business and the crowd begins to rush in. Costco estimates that one-third of members who visit a warehouse make a purchase at a Food Court. After lunch, the morning crew winds down and the relief crew preps for the dinner rush, thawing and proofing more pizza dough. When the warehouse closes, a 4-5 person crew cleans up and closes.

ENSALADA COBB 3,99

TIM ROSE

In 2022, after 39 years of service, Tim Rose, one of Costco's founding officers, retired as the Executive Vice President, Ancillary Businesses, Manufacturing, and Business Centers.

Tim was an assistant general manager at the first Costco (Seattle #01), then opened the Tacoma warehouse in 1984. Two years later, he transferred to the Home Office and was involved in the development of the fresh foods and Kirkland Signature businesses.

Tim was also pivotal in the Food Court's success.

ARE THERE DIFFERENCES OVERSEAS?

Every Costco Food Court sells hot dogs, soda, and pizza, but the rest of the menu is ever-changing, with interesting regional and seasonal variations around the world!

AUSTRALIA

INDIAN-STYLE BUTTER CHICKEN PIE

CLAM CHOWDER IN A BREAD BOWL

KOREAN CHICKEN RIBS

TARO TEA

OR

MANGO SMOOTHIE WITH BOBA

ICELAND

CRISPY ONIONS AS A TOPPING FOR HOT DOGS

PARIS

SURPRISINGLY, FISH-AND-CHIPS

MEXICO

MANGO SMOOTHIES

UNLIMITED JALAPEÑO PEPPERS TO GARNISH HOT DOGS

MONTRÉAL

POUTINE (CHEESE CURDS, GRAVY, AND FRENCH FRIES)

TAIWAN

CLAM CHOWDER

HAWAIIAN PIZZA

CRISPY SPICY CHICKEN

UK

"JACKET POTATOES" WITH A CHOICE OF TOPPINGS (TUNA, BAKED BEANS, CHEESE, OR BEEF CHILI)

KOREA

BULGOGI BEEF PIZZA

MUSHROOM SOUP

JAPAN

CORN CHOWDER

FALAFEL SALAD

SOFT SERVE ICE CREAM

FRANCE

THE FIRST FRENCH WAREHOUSE
HAD SOME "WOW" ITEMS INDEED:
SMART CARS, CAVIAR, AND A
15-LITER BOTTLE OF CHAMPAGNE!
VOILÀ!

WHY DID IT TAKE SO LONG FOR COSTCO TO OPEN IN FRANCE?

Soon after Costco expanded into the UK, in 1993, they wanted to open in France and Spain. But the company was already busy expanding in Asia, and the thicket of EU regulations was off-putting, so it took more than twenty years for the French expansion. Jim Sinegal's son Michael, after helping to open and run Costco in Japan, relocated to the land of wine and cheese to advance Costco's French experience. A significant number of employees from the French-speaking province of Québec, Canada were also deployed. France is highly unionized, so there were special preparations for workers. On June 22, 2017, Costco finally opened its first French warehouse, in Villebon-sur-Yvette, a Paris suburb. Five years later, on December 4, 2021, Costco opened another warehouse, in the Les Quatres Chênes shopping mall in Pontault Combault, 14 miles east of Paris.

ARE THERE ANY SUSTAINABILITY FEATURES OF THE FRENCH WAREHOUSES?

The warehouses have almost one-third more green space than required, offer free charging stations for electric vehicles, optimize natural lighting to reduce the amount of artificial lighting, and use recovered rainwater in compliance with *Haute Qualité Environmentale* (High Environmental Standards). Water and energy meters, and improved fittings, are also relied upon to optimize energy consumption.

IS THERE ANYTHING UNUSUAL ABOUT THE FRENCH WAREHOUSES?

Perhaps the most striking feature of the Villebon warehouse is the *mur vivant* — a large hydroponic living wall. The French warehouses use an electronic device to scan membership cards upon entry, and also on the Food Court beverage dispensers to limit refills of sugared drinks — a system we haven't seen elsewhere. In a nod to the prevalence of the many superb *boulangeries* and *patisseries* (bakeries and pastry shops) throughout France, the Bakery department is a bit smaller than in an American warehouse and sells standard items like cookies and muffins as well as French specialties like *madeleines*, *mini-beignets*, and *pain au chocolat*. The cheese selection is staggering in quality and pricing. For example, a sampler of four Burgundy cheeses, including both Epoisses and Brillat-Savarin, were priced at less than $20 in November 2022 — a *prix fantastique!*

WHAT IS ON LE MENU AT THE FOOD COURT?

The Food Court has the standard Costco hot dog/soda combo, plus items that are found in the UK like chicken tenders, French fries, and fish-and-chips. Instead of all-beef hamburgers, there are ground chicken burgers, available with *pommes frites* (French fries). For dessert there is a very American ice cream sundae and a very French *gaufre choco noisette chantilly*, which is a marvelous combination of waffles, chocolate sauce, nuts, and whipped cream. *Bon Appétit!*

ANY NOTEWORTHY NON-FOOD ITEMS FOR SALE?

A 53-inch plush Teddy Bear sold out quickly at the opening, and is still very popular. The French are very *sportif* (athletically inclined) so there is a wide range of high-end fitness options, from treadmills, Nordic Tracks, and rowing machines for adults, to air hockey and an E-Z-fold basketball arcade for kids, plus bicycles for all ages.

F

HOW ARE THE FRENCH WAREHOUSES SUPPLIED?

Buyers for Costco in Europe are headquartered in the UK, but there are also regional French buyers who specialize in local products. The main logistics hub is also in the UK, although some goods are trucked directly from vendors in France to the French warehouses. The long-range plan is to have a few more warehouses close to Paris and near other large cities, so it is possible that France may eventually have its own logistics and depot system.

HOW IS THE LIQUOR SELECTION?

Naturally, there is an overwhelming assortment of French wines and Champagnes, especially Bordeaux, Burgundies, Côtes-du-Rhône, Châteauneuf-du-Papes, local French vintages, and wines from other European countries. For many of these varieties there are Kirkland Signature counterparts, often made by well-known vintners. Kirkland Signature French Vodka is available worldwide. When we visited in 2022, the wine display cases featured a number of Costco-sized and Costco-priced bottles of amazing vintages for sale, like a Balthazar of Veuve Clicquot for about $1,600, which was a great deal.

ARE THERE ANY NOTABLE FRESH FOOD ITEMS?

The Deli section is chock-full of French favorites like a large platter of Kirkland Signature Beef Bour-guignon for a very reasonable $14; two very large Kirkland Signature Croque Monsieur sandwiches for $11; or a large platter of *choucroute garnie* for $16. There are hot, roasted Kirkland Signature *jarrets de porc chaud* (pork knuckles) — right next to Costco's famous rotisserie chicken — and a burrata salad. The fresh meat, poultry, and fish selections are local and noteworthy in variety. The Deli section also has a lovely selection of French macarons, mousses, crème brulé, and flan.

JEWELRY AND HANDBAGS ARE QUITE POPULAR AT FRENCH COSTCO WAREHOUSES. ON OPENING DAY, THE FIRST WAREHOUSE SOLD A ONE-OF-A-KIND NECKLACE WORTH $352,400!

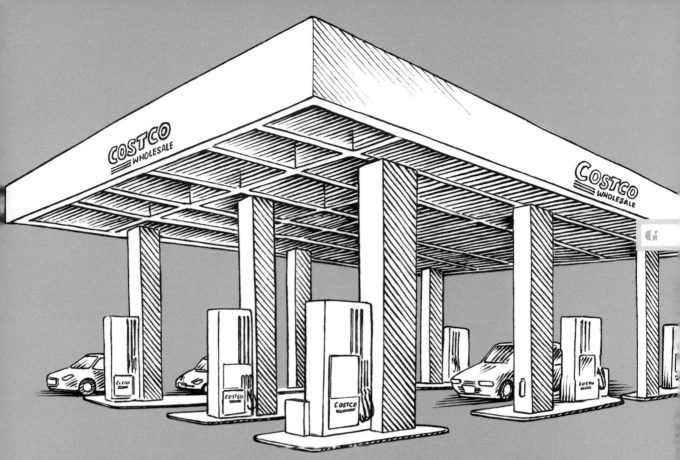

GASOLINE
& CAR WASHES

IN 2020, COSTCO SOLD
$14.7 BILLION WORTH OF GAS
— AT A WHOPPING 21 CENTS
BELOW THE COMPETITION

HOW DID COSTCO GET INTO THE GASOLINE BUSINESS?

FedMart, Costco's predecessor, sold *premium* gas only a few cents above the price of *regular,* hoping to draw customers into the store. In 1973, FedMart even set up its own wholesale gas supplier to weather oil shortages during the energy crisis. Later on, Price Club was less successful competing against the oil-company-owned gas stations, which controlled the price of gas from the refinery to the pump. In 1995, Rick Libenson and Dennis Zook persuaded Jim Sinegal and Jeff Brotman to sell gas at Costco, opening their first two fuel stations, in Arizona (Scottsdale and Tucson). The timing was perfect: gas prices were soaring and Costco offered gas at significantly lower prices than local stations, attracting intense local media attention in the process. Plus, for every dollar of gas pumped at a Costco fuel station, members purchased, on average, an additional 70 cents inside the warehouse.

COSTCO HAS CAR WASH FACILITIES, TOO?

On April 26, 2006, Costco opened its first car wash at the South Seattle warehouse, priced well below most competitors. Costco members can also get a car wash at select warehouses in Arizona, California, Idaho, Tennessee, and Washington. Costco car washes use special foam brushes, which are cleaner, quieter, and less likely to scratch a car's finish, and use, on average, no more than 40 gallons of water — less than a typical load of home laundry. All the water at a Costco car wash is either recycled or returned to the environment cleanly.

HOW MUCH GASOLINE DOES COSTCO SELL?

In 2020, with only 615 gas stations worldwide — mainly in the US — gas accounted for 9% of Costco's total sales. Costco doesn't offer gas in Korea or China; in other countries, the number of stations varies widely due to local restrictions or lack of space. Costco sells top-grade Tier One gas and is active in the forward market to benefit both members and their own truck operations. Costco customers are repeat shoppers in ways that customers of other gasoline chains are not.

GOOD WORKS

COSTCO CONTRIBUTES TO A WIDE VARIETY OF LOCAL, NATIONAL, AND GLOBAL CHARITABLE CAUSES

COSTCO MAKES A POSITIVE CONTRIBUTION TO COMMUNITIES WHERE THEY DO BUSINESS: SUPPORTING CHILDREN, EDUCATION, HEALTH AND HUMAN SERVICES, AND DISASTER RELIEF.*

DOES COSTCO DONATE FOOD?

Costco is very discriminating about freshness and culls edible but not perfect items for donation to local food banks, among other beneficiaries. For example, at the Food Court, pizza and similar items are only sold for a limited time after they are prepared; these "unsellable" items are then frozen and donated. In 2018 alone, Costco donated 37 million meals to Feeding America, a national organization which works with local food banks. Through these donations, Costco also saves money that would otherwise be spent on hauling and garbage collection fees, savings that are passed along to members.

WHAT IS THE ORIGIN OF COSTCO'S COMMITMENT TO CHARITABLE GIVING?

Since his FedMart days in the 1950s, Sol Price was always committed to giving back to the community, and encouraged his employees to do the same, a tradition energetically continued by Costco with its culture of giving. The annual Workplace Giving campaign enables Costco employees to support their favorite causes with donations to 501(c)(3) not-for-profit organizations, which Costco will match up to 60%. In 2021, the campaign raised $31.7 million for thousands of worthy causes including places of worship, schools, animal shelters, and disaster relief.

DOES COSTCO PROVIDE EDUCATIONAL SCHOLARSHIPS?

Costco funds scholarships through the College Success Foundation. As of March 2023, there is a national scholarship program for which all Costco employees — full and part-time — are eligible to apply, and another program, the Costco Scholarship Fund, which targets under-represented students of color at either the University of Washington or Seattle University.

*Suffice it to say, this list of Costco's good works is not comprehensive.

HOW DOES COSTCO SUPPORT CHILDREN'S MIRACLE NETWORK?

Costco sponsors an annual campaign for the Children's Miracle Network Hospitals (CMNH), a Utah-based not-for-profit that supports a network of children's hospitals in the US and Canada. The fund-raiser involves selling CMNH balloons for one dollar each, which allows broad participation. In 2022, the 35th anniversary of Costco's association with CMNH, Costco employees and members donated $36 million and Costco contributed an additional $7.6 million to raise a total of $43.6 million. An example of how this support has been meaningful: in Honolulu, Costco helped fund a maternity wing for the Kapiolani Medical Center for Women and Children, part of the CMNH network.

DOES COSTCO RESTRICT ITS GOOD WORKS TO ORGANIZED NOT-FOR-PROFITS?

In addition to major contributions to organized not-for-profit charities, Costco helps out informally at the local level, particularly during the immediate aftermath of a natural disaster; then, Costco donates staples like food, apparel, water, and paper goods to help those affected. In the Christmas season, employees in many warehouses work together to donate money for gifts and other items for needy families in the area. In Africa, Costco has worked directly with small communities of farmers to build schools and health facilities.

WHAT IS WORLD VISION?

Costco gives vendors the opportunity to donate merchandise returned by members to World Vision International, a not-for-profit that supports needy communities around the world. In 2020, Costco donated 54,000 pallets of first-quality goods to World Vision for use in 32 countries — merchandise which otherwise would have been destroyed or returned to vendors, like office chairs that might find their way to Zambia or bikes which might end up in El Salvador. World Vision also sends donations for disaster relief efforts such as water, diapers, blankets, and generators. The relationship was launched as a pilot program at the Sumner, Washington depot, but now all return depots donate to World Vision.

HALAL

MANY COSTCO WAREHOUSES SELL HALAL FOOD

WHAT IS "HALAL" FOOD?

The Muslim faith divides all activities into "halal" (permitted) and "haram" (prohibited). Based on the Koran, halal is a broad term most often associated with food. The laws are far more complex than can be summarized here, but some practices may be familiar even to non-Muslims: no pork or any product from pigs, and no alcohol. Methods for slaughtering animals for food are strictly prescribed.

DOES COSTCO SELL HALAL FOOD?

In areas with significant Muslim communities, Costco sells packaged meats including halal poultry, steak, ground beef, cubed goat meat, and ground lamb. In some warehouses, whole halal lambs and goats from New Zealand can be found in the freezer units.

HOW CAN SOMEONE BE SURE THAT FOOD LABELLED HALAL IS INDEED HALAL?

In the US, there are at least twelve recognized halal certifiers; among them are the Islamic Food and Nutrition Council of America (IFANCA), based in Des Plaines, Illinois, and the American Halal Foundation, headquartered in Tampa, Florida. The former marks its certified products with a crescent moon; the latter uses an eight-pointed star with a capital H inside. In the absence of halal certification, some Islamic authorities consider kosher food to be an acceptable replacement, so snacks like Hershey's chocolate and Chobani yogurt — as well as over 800 Kirkland Signature products certified kosher by the Orthodox Union — would also be considered halal. [SEE "KOSHER"]

HOW BIG IS THE HALAL FOOD MARKET?

In 2022, with a world-wide population of about 900 million Muslims, experts estimated the global halal market at $2 trillion. The five countries with the largest Muslim populations are Indonesia, Pakistan, India, Bangladesh, and Nigeria. In contrast, the US has some 3.3 million Muslims, the UK has 2.1 million, and Sweden, 700,000. About 60% of American Muslims live in three cities: New York, Chicago, and Los Angeles.

HAWAII

IN 2022, IWILEI SALES
EXCEEDED $500 MILLION — THE
FIRST COSTCO TO DO SO

HOW SUCCESSFUL IS HONOLULU'S IWILEI COSTCO WAREHOUSE?

Although average in size, Iwilei is known as the Big Kahuna because it accounts for about 25% of Hawaii's total sales and regularly ranks among the top five busiest Costco warehouses in the world. This single location often does more than 7,000 transactions each day — about twice the Costco average — at more than $200 per shopping cart. More than forty SKUs at this one warehouse sell over $1 million per year. One holiday season, Iwilei Meat sales reached $1.5 million in a single week, with over $400,000 of meat sold on *one day.* A handful of warehouses come close to being this busy — including one in Maui — but no other warehouse regularly beats Iwilei.

WHEN AND WHY DID COSTCO EXPAND TO THE ALOHA STATE?

Hawaii has a high cost of living, limited competition, a resident population of 1.4 million, ten million visitors each year, and leads the US in multigenerational households (about one in five) due to chronic housing shortages and cultural influences. In 1988, having successfully expanded to Alaska, Jim Sinegal and Jeff Brotman opened the first Hawaiian Costco in the Salt Lake neighborhood of Honolulu. In 2002, that warehouse was moved from Salt Lake to Iwilei. The seven Hawaiian warehouses are part of Costco's Los Angeles region, with about two-thirds of merchandise shipped from California in a journey that takes only five days — about the same amount of time required for produce to travel by truck across the US.

THE FRESH FISH AND SEAFOOD IN HAWAII ARE AMAZING; WHAT'S ON OFFER AT THE COSTCO WAREHOUSE?

While beef and pork are the same as on the mainland, the locally sourced seafood is very different: crab, lobster, ahi tuna, and ahi sashimi from the Pacific are plentiful, along with an impressive array of fresh wild fish — ono, swordfish, blue marlin, black cod, and more. Calamari steaks can be found in the frozen seafood section. There are also multiple kinds of fresh poke daily — we enjoyed them all!

ANY NON-FOOD ITEMS OF NOTE?

Not surprisingly, products related to the beach — surf boards, boogie boards, swim gear — and outdoor hobbies like golf, camping, and barbecuing are well-represented. We were delighted to buy Costco-themed Hawaiian shirts, adorned with the names and illustrations of the state's various warehouse locations. Hawaiian Costco warehouses sell magnificent fresh orchid leis in the flower section.

IS COSTCO'S HAWAIIAN PRODUCE LOCALLY SOURCED? ANYTHING UNIQUE?

Costco Hawaii sells only Maui Gold pineapples, sweeter and lower in acidity, which are best eaten fresh; unfortunately, they are not well-suited to canning. You might enjoy hand-cut fresh pineapple slices with Li Hing Mui seasoning (a dried plum powder that is simultaneously sweet, sour, and salty) or whole pineapples. Costco also sells apple bananas, a local specialty. Named for their slight apple-like aroma, apple bananas are sweet, short, and plump with a slight tang; they retain their firm texture longer than standard bananas, and are usually only sold at farmers markets. There are several Japanese produce varieties that are locally grown (e.g., cucumbers, eggplants, and Kabocha squash). Other unusual items are purple sweet potatoes and 3½-pound bags of poi, a taro-based paste which is an important part of the traditional Hawaiian diet.

WHAT ABOUT LOCAL VENDORS?

About 50 Hawaiian vendors supply more than 220 edible SKUs to Costco. Hawaiians will generally support a local producer if the product is high quality and not much more expensive than a mainland brand. In Honolulu, we had the chance to visit Hawaiian King, a premiere confectioner founded in 1978, where we watched production of — and sampled! — hand-manufactured candy, chocolate, and other treats, much of it including delicious local macadamia nuts. Eggs have always played an important role in the Hawaiian diet as a low-cost, versatile protein, but until 2021 most were imported from the mainland. We toured the off-grid, cage-free, sustainable Villa Rose Egg Farm on the north shore of Oahu. The eggs are a bit more expensive than the ones shipped from Arizona, but very popular.

PINEAPPLE PLANTS DO NOT BEAR FRUIT UNTIL THEY ARE AT LEAST 18 MONTHS OLD AND THEN BEAR ONLY ONE FRUIT.

HOW DID COSTCO BEGIN WORKING WITH HONOLULU COOKIE COMPANY?

Established in 1998, Honolulu Cookie Company is famous for its shortbread cookies in the shape of a pineapple, symbolizing hospitality. During the pandemic, this family-owned cookie manufacturer with many high-end retail shops in Hawaii was in peril when the tourist trade evaporated. Costco began selling their extraordinary product, with pricing even better than duty-free shopping, and now sells this popular brand around the world.

HAWAII IS FAMOUS FOR ITS COFFEE — WHAT IS SOLD AT COSTCO?

The Hawaiian warehouses offer coffee from three different islands: Molokai, Kauai, and Kona. Costco sources its Kona coffee from Mamalahoa Estate, a coffee farm owned by long-time Costco vendor San Francisco Bay Coffee. The farm is situated between 500 and 1,500 feet above the ocean on the west coast of the Big Island, about 30 miles south of the Kona Airport. The climate and soil are ideal for growing these special coffee beans, which can sell for up to $35 per pound. The farm combines traditional coffee agriculture, handpicking every bean, with the most advanced technology for processing and roasting.

WHAT'S THE STORY WITH HAWAII AND SPAM?

Spam was first introduced in Hawaii during World War II, served to GIs on military bases, and soon became an island favorite, often served fried with rice or in a form of sushi called Spam musubi. Costco sells *a lot* of it: in 2022, just two SKUs (regular and low sodium) in only seven warehouses accounted for about $7 million in sales.

COSTCO
IS RATED #1
FOR
HEARING AIDS
BY CONSUMER
REPORTS, AND AT
A FRACTION
OF THE COST OF
MOST OTHER
PLACES!

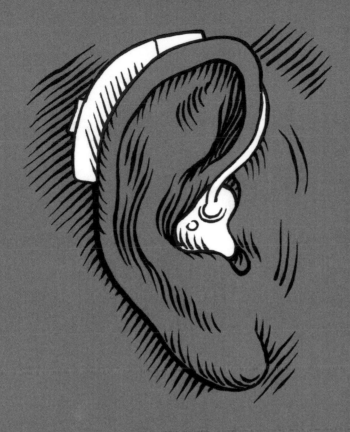

HEARING AIDS

WHAT'S THAT YOU SAY? COSTCO SELLS HEARING AIDS?

You betcha! Unless you happen to be a US veteran, there's probably no better place to get hearing aids than at Costco. The US Veterans Administration is the only other larger source. (The VA provides 20% of all hearing aids in the US.) Otherwise, Costco is the dominant player and negotiates great prices, which they pass along to members. As of November, 2022, Costco's Hearing Center was selling three major brands — Jabra, Philips, and Rexton — for up to $6,000 less than a private audiologist. Costco Hearing Center employees are not paid on a commission basis.

WHAT'S THE PROJECTED GROWTH OF THE HEARING AID MARKET?

The global hearing aid market, estimated at $8.4 billion in 2020, is expected to almost double by 2026, to $14.5 billion, due to rising life expectancy and lifestyle choices. Approximately 48 million Americans have some form of hearing loss, mostly older adults. Almost one-third of those over 65 have disabling hearing loss, which increases to 50% by age 75, with men almost twice as likely as women to have hearing loss. Hearing loss can lead to a 30-40% increase in an accelerated rate of cognitive decline and depression as a result of social withdrawal and isolation. Those with at least a 25-decibel hearing loss are three times more likely to report a fall. According to the NIH, almost 30 million Americans aged 20-69 could benefit from hearing aids.

IS MEMBERSHIP REQUIRED TO USE THE COSTCO HEARING CENTER?

At Costco, anyone — members and non-members alike — can get a free hearing test by a licensed audiologist; at a private audiologist, the test could cost up to $350. Although you don't need a Costco membership for the hearing test, you will need an appointment — and must be a member to actually purchase hearing aids. You can bring a prescription from another provider or get one from Costco after a hearing test; prescriptions are only valid for 90 days.

ARE THERE ANY OTHER PERKS TO GETTING HEARING AIDS AT COSTCO BESIDES THE HIGH QUALITY AT A LOW PRICE?

Costco offers free cleaning, check-ups, and follow-up appointments, as well as a two-year loss and damage protection policy with no deductible. The purchase price also includes a standard three-year Costco warranty covering any repairs that may be required, including replacement of the hearing aid, if necessary. We were delighted to have a hearing aid, purchased at Costco in New York City, repaired for free, without an appointment, at a Costco warehouse in Seoul, Korea, with no questions asked. If you are not satisfied with any purchase at Costco, including your membership or your new hearing aids, you can get a full refund. Even if you don't get hearing aids at Costco, the Kirkland Signature batteries sell for a fraction of the price at most national drugstore chains. (Although the current trend seems to be away from battery-powered hearing aids toward rechargeables.)

HEARING AIDS ARE NOW AVAILABLE OVER THE COUNTER — WHY WOULD I NEED A PRESCRIPTION?

As of October 2022, a hearing test and prescription were no longer required by the FDA — for adults aged 18 and older with perceived mild or moderate hearing loss — to buy certain types of hearing aids over the counter. However, purchasing hearing aids from a hearing health professional such as those at Costco allows for fitting and adjustments to the device based on individual hearing loss and ear structure.

I HEARD...

Hearing aids potentially stave off cognitive decline and social withdrawal, «(and also increase the range at which you can eavesdrop on others' conversations!)»

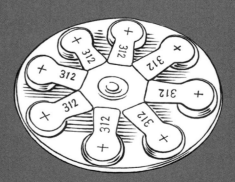

HOT DOGS

COSTCO SELLS SEVEN TIMES
MORE HOT DOGS THAN ALL MLB
STADIUMS *COMBINED*

HOW ABOUT A TASTE OF THE HOT DOG'S HISTORY?

It dates back to Ancient Greece, when sausages were mentioned in *The Odyssey*. By the 13th century, Germany and Austria had both laid claim to the delicacy, calling them "frankfurters" and "wieners," respectively. In the 1800s, German immigrants to the US dubbed them "dachshund dogs." In 1893, they were popular at the Chicago World's Fair. In 1916, Nathan's Famous began selling them for five cents apiece, and later sponsored the first international hot dog eating contest. In 2014, the National Hot Dog and Sausage Council estimated that on a typical Fourth of July, Americans consume 150 million hot dogs — enough to span the US five times!

THE PRICE OF THE
HOT DOG AND BEVERAGE AT COSTCO
HAS NOT CHANGED
SINCE 1985

WHEN DID COSTCO START SELLING HOT DOGS?

Around 1984, both Price Club and Costco began selling them, but Price Club was first. At the San Diego Price Club, Rick Libenson and Roman Braun, Price Club's senior food merchant, purchased hot dogs from Hebrew National — and got a cart for free. Costco began selling hot dogs soon after in Portland, when warehouse manager Joe Portera agreed to let a vendor nicknamed "Warm Wonderful Gene" set up a cart. Unaware they were making history, Gene and Joe agreed on a price of $1.50 for a hot dog *and* a can of soda. Jim Sinegal and Jeff Brotman visited the Portland warehouse a short time later and chided Joe for not first consulting with the Home Office, but Jeff loved the hot dog and all was forgiven. [SEE "FOOD COURT"]

DIFFERENT TOPPINGS AROUND THE WORLD:

KETCHUP, MUSTARD, AND RELISH
Most Food Courts have ketchup, mustard, and relish.

FRIED CRISPY ONIONS
In Iceland, fried crispy onions (the kind used in green bean casserole) are a unique popular topping.

CUSTOM "KIMCHI"
In South Korea, members create their own "kimchi" to use as a garnish, combining raw onions, ketchup, and mustard.

PICKLED JALAPEÑO PEPPERS
In Mexico, pickled jalapeño peppers are offered in large, hand-cranked dispensers.

WHO MAKES COSTCO'S HOT DOGS?

Originally, kosher all-beef hot dogs were sourced mainly from Hebrew National and Best Sinai; in Chicago, the Lincoln Park Costco was sourced by the Vienna plant next door. In 1993, Conagra bought Hebrew National and Sara Lee bought Best Sinai and both started raising the price of hot dogs, but Costco kept their price at $1.50 for the combo. In 2008, Craig Jelinek approached Jim about possibly increasing the price, and Jim reportedly replied: "If you raise the effing hot dog [price], I will kill you. Go figure it out!" So in 2009, Costco built its first meat processing plant near Stockton, California — and then another southwest of Chicago — to manufacture their own hot dogs. Both facilities are spotlessly clean, co-located with existing depots, and ship around the world. The Kirkland Signature hot dogs are "one-quarter-pound-plus": larger than the original dogs, but no longer kosher. (In the Asia Pacific region, the hot dogs are all pork.)

WILL COSTCO EVER RAISE THE PRICE OF ITS $1.50 HOT DOG AND SODA?

Not on your life, according to Jim's legendary reply to a *Seattle Times* reporter who asked when Costco would increase the price: "When I'm dead!" As Craig explained at an Issaquah Chamber of Commerce luncheon in April, 2022, "By having the discipline to say, 'You are not going to be able to raise your price. You have to figure it out,' we took it over and started manufacturing our own hot dogs. We keep it at $1.50 and make enough money to get a fair return." In 2022, the price of the soda on its own was increased by a dime, but the combo price remains unchanged.

WHICH COSTCO FOOD COURT SELLS THE MOST HOT DOGS?

During the busiest four-week period in late 2012, the Costco warehouse in Shin Misato, Japan, sold a whopping 64,512 hot dog and soda combinations, followed by Iwilei, Hawaii with 55,000 combos — dwarfing the US warehouse average of 13,500 in the same period. More recent numbers may vary, but these two warehouses are always in the top ten for global Costco hot dog/soda combo sales.

75%
OF THE
POPULATION
ARE
COSTCO
MEMBERS

ICELAND

I KNOW THAT ICELAND HAS VOLCANOES AND WATERFALLS, BUT THERE'S A COSTCO, TOO?

On May 23, 2017, Costco opened a warehouse in Garðabær (population: 16,300), a municipality six miles south of Iceland's capital, Reykjavik. The opening was Costco's biggest since arriving in Europe in 1993: 40,000 members signed up *before the warehouse even opened*. There's a Costco in Iceland Facebook group, with 97,000 members — about a quarter of the country's population, which in the US would be equivalent to 86 *million* members.

HOW DOES MERCHANDISE GET TO THE ICELAND WAREHOUSE?

Costco originally intended to supply the warehouse from North America; however, due to EU import regulations, UK sourcing made more sense financially and logistically. Merchandise is either trucked from the British depot and shipped from the port at Immingham, or sent by fast ferry and air from Europe via Rotterdam. Fortunately, when the UK left the EU in early 2020, Iceland was one of the first EU countries to negotiate a bilateral trade agreement with the UK, so the sourcing was unchanged by Brexit. Fresh fish and meat are sourced exclusively from Iceland because imports are prohibited by law.

WHY DID COSTCO DECIDE TO OPEN IN ICELAND?

In 2007, Joe Portera, Costco EVP for Eastern and Canadian Divisions, noticed hundreds of shrink-wrapped pallets in the loading bay at the warehouse in St. John's, Newfoundland, Canada. He investigated and learned that twice a year, a group from Iceland rented a stripped-down Boeing 737 jet, loaded it up with Costco merchandise — primarily Kirkland Signature items — and resold the goods with a markup close to 100%. Joe informed the Home Office and suggested that Costco open a warehouse themselves, even though it would be too small to support its own management team. Importantly, Iceland helped Costco test whether or not a small country could be managed remotely.

WHY IS COSTCO SO SUCCESSFUL IN ICELAND?

Iceland is an isolated island country with a small population and a barren landscape, so it has always relied on imported goods, resulting in high prices. In 2016, the year before Costco opened in Iceland, food prices were almost 50% higher than in the rest of the EU. Costco was able to bring high-quality products to the Icelandic consumer at significantly lower prices than those offered by Iceland's own supermarket chains, which drove their prices down — a phenomenon dubbed the "Costco effect." Icelanders like Americans. During WWII, Iceland was an important Allied base. US troops remained for decades after the war; Icelanders got to know Americans and adopted some of their traditions, like barbecuing. Most Icelanders have a grill in the backyard or on an apartment terrace, which is used year-round! When Costco arrived on the scene, it set off a frenzy.

ARE THERE ANY UNIQUE PRODUCTS OR FEATURES?

The Iceland warehouse has a green lawn on its roof as a reference to traditional Icelandic turf houses, which relied on sod for insulation from the harsh northern climates. For barbecuing, Costco in Iceland sells a wide variety of marinated meats and barbecue sauces. Two items of note at the Food Court: crispy onions as a topping for hot dogs and gelato imported from Italy. In 2020, Costco in the UK and Iceland began selling gold ingots sourced from Baird & Co, the largest gold refiner in the UK.

JAPAN'S HAMAMATSU COSTCO HOLDS THE RECORD FOR FIRST DAY OPENING SALES, AT MORE THAN $4.95 MILLION

JAPAN

WHY DID IT TAKE UNTIL 1999 FOR COSTCO TO OPEN IN JAPAN?

When Costco opened in South Korea (1994) and Taiwan (1997), they worked with domestic partners. In Japan, this process was a particular challenge. Jim Sinegal recalls one potential partner who, after many meetings, politely conceded that they had no intention of working with Costco — only because they were asked directly! By 1999, Jim's son Michael, along with Ken Theriault, a senior Costco executive from Canada, were tasked with the expansion. They persuaded senior management to open without a local partner. Another challenge was *Daitenho*, a Japanese law which allowed an existing business to object to a similar business opening nearby. In 1999, having successfully overcome all *Daitenho* objections, Costco opened its first Japanese warehouse in Hisayama, a suburb of the southern port city of Fukuoka. (Soon after, *Daitenho* was relaxed.) As of May 2023, Japan has 32 warehouses, with many more expected.

HOW IS THE FISH AND SEAFOOD SELECTION IN JAPANESE COSTCOS?

Fresh food accounts for almost 30% of sales in Japan (versus 15% in the US), about 65% locally sourced. The typical Japanese Costco fish selection is much larger than in the US, and dwarfs the Japanese Meat department, too. The choices are incredible, including yellowtail jaw or loin filets, fresh salmon roe, salted cod, three kinds of mackerel, lobster tails, short-neck clams, cooked octopus, Argentine shrimp, frozen squid, and several kinds of fresh seaweed. There is also *a lot* of sushi, which members can watch being prepared. Two tempting sushi items are a 48-count tray for the equivalent of about $23, and a mouth-watering, family-sized, colorful chirashi platter. Sushi is sold within two hours of preparation; inventory is carefully managed to prevent leftovers at the end of the day.

ANYTHING STRUCTURALLY UNIQUE ABOUT THE JAPANESE COSTCO WAREHOUSES?

A typical US warehouse occupies 18-20 acres on only one level. Almost 75% of Japan is uninhabitably mountainous and the remainder is very densely populated. Large parcels of land are rare and often owned by syndicates composed of individual plot owners represented by a single landlord. Costco must be creative, often creating multi-level warehouses with giant moving ramps to ferry members from floor to floor, and pallet elevators for merchandise. Steel pilings, driven deep below the ground, provide extra stabilization to improve earthquake resistance. [SEE "EMERGENCIES"]

DOES COSTCO CATER TO JAPAN'S LOVE OF BASEBALL?

The Hiroshima warehouse abuts the Mazda Zoom-Zoom Stadium, home to the Toyo Carp baseball team. There's a great view of the field from the warehouse's rooftop parking lot. On game days, Costco limits parking time so members do not have to compete with baseball fans who want to watch the game for free, parking included. The Hiroshima Food Court is larger than others in Japan, correctly anticipating that baseball games drive higher sales, especially for hot dogs.

ARE THERE ANCILLARY BUSINESSES?

Costco in Japan offers Optical, Pharmacy, and Hearing Centers just like in the US. Notably, prescription lenses are cut right in the optical department of each warehouse — in only thirty minutes — instead of relying on the US optical fulfillment centers.

ANY SPECIAL ACTIVITIES ON OPENING DAY FOR A WAREHOUSE IN JAPAN?

In addition to the traditional ribbon-cutting, there may also be a *Kagami Biraki* ("opening the lid") ceremony during which wooden mallets are used to break open the tops of large wooden barrels of *iwai-zake* (celebration sake), to represent breaking open good fortune. The sake is then shared among those present. These celebratory sake barrels — empty — are on display in regional offices around Japan.

HOW SUCCESSFUL HAS COSTCO BEEN IN JAPAN?

Although Costco's arrival in Japan was protested by some major competitors, Costco has caught on in a big way. Costco believes that, with a country population of 126 million people, there is enormous growth potential for the company in Japan. The country is already served by two domestic depots, which provide infrastructure for significant expansion. As of September 2022, four more sites were "green inked." [SEE "LINGO"] Within the next ten years, plans are to double the number of Japanese Costco warehouses to a total of sixty.

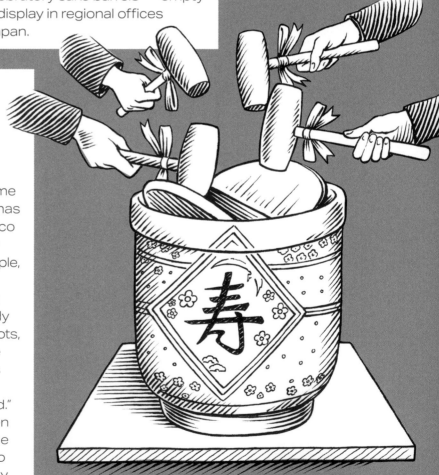

IS THE FOOD COURT THE SAME AS IN THE US?

Japan is often the top-seller of the $1.50 hot dog/soda combo in the world, but that hot dog is pork rather than beef. [SEE "HOT DOGS"] You can also get a bucket of chicken nuggets and French fries, clam chowder, or bulgogi-topped pizza. Soft ice cream flavors rotate throughout the year and include exotic flavors like mango and green tea. The Food Court sells a delicious mango smoothie year-round.

SHIN MISATO BAKERY IS 2½ TIMES THE SIZE OF THE AVERAGE US COSTCO BAKERY

HOW DO BAKERY, PRODUCE, AND OTHER FOODS COMPARE TO THE US?

Bakery and Wine & Spirits occupy vast swaths of any Japanese warehouse, with plenty of sake and other Asian spirits. Usually, there is an entire aisle of rice, with 22-pound bags for only $20. When Costco opened in Japan, management was incorrectly advised that American baked goods would not be popular. Yet Costco Japan sells the same baked goods as in the US — plus a delicious Earl Grey Tea muffin — and has achieved the largest Bakery penetration in the Costco system. In fact, the Japanese Bakeries must work literally around the clock to meet demand, in bakeries that are often much larger than in the US. Produce like sea asparagus, Japanese cucumbers, a massive variety of domestic mushrooms, and fresh corn [SEE "ZAMA"] are sourced locally, displayed alongside California strawberries and Peruvian avocados. US-sourced merchandise is shipped from the Mira Loma, California depot, which serves the Los Angeles region. Snack items are largely domestic, and include a wide range of unique treats that would be difficult to find in the US.

Costco

JEWELRY

IN 2021, COSTCO SOLD 475,000 CARATS OF DIAMONDS — ABOUT 212 POUNDS

HOW DID COSTCO GET STARTED IN THE JEWELRY BUSINESS?

In 1954, Sol Price and his colleagues Leo Freedman and Mandell Weiss started FedMart, the precursor to Costco. Leo and Mandell were jewelers by trade, so they decided the store would be an ideal location for a jewelry concession. Early on, jewelry contributed significantly to FedMart's success, and has been a part of the business model ever since.

HOW MUCH JEWELRY DOES COSTCO SELL?

Over the past few years, total sales of jewelry and fine watches have hovered around $1.6 billion, which ranks Costco fourth on the *National Jeweler* magazine's $100 Million Super-sellers List, just behind Signet, Walmart, and Amazon. Jewelry is usually one of the top-selling warehouse departments per square foot of display space.

DOES ANYBODY REALLY BUY FINE JEWELRY AT A COSTCO WAREHOUSE?

In 2009, national television news coverage of the opening of the Manhattan Costco warehouse mentioned an extremely rare pink diamond ring valued at well over $200,000. A Chicago viewer, who must have known that pink diamonds account for only 0.1% of the 20 million carats of diamonds mined each year, called to purchase it. And a Costco member once bought a 10-carat cushion cut solitaire diamond engagement ring for $600,000! Diamonds greater than one carat are sold with a Gemological Institute of America certification — considered the gold standard of gemological certification — regarding the "four c's": carat, cut, clarity, and color. (For security, some items on display are replicas.)

WHAT IS COSTO'S POLICY WITH RESPECT TO "BLOOD DIAMONDS?"

Costco checks vendors to confirm that funds generated by the sale of diamonds don't finance local or regional conflicts, and that workers who mine the gems are not exploited. Costco also keeps tabs on the sources of gold used in its jewelry, checking the labor practices of the gold mines. In fact, Costco conducts "social audits" of vendors for ethical business practices. [SEE "VENDORS"]

DO INTERNATIONAL JEWELRY SECTIONS DIFFER FROM THOSE IN THE US?

Since the beginning of the pandemic in 2020, regional overseas buyers thought economic uncertainties might increase the demand for inflation-resistant assets like gold and silver. In the UK, Iceland, Sweden, and Asia, gold and silver ingots and bullion coins are also sold in the jewelry cases. As of December, 2022, a 500-gram bar of Baird 24k gold sold for about $31,000 in Stockholm; in Zama, Japan, a 100-gram bar of 24k gold sold for about $6,600. (Due to fluctuations in pricing, precious metals are non-returnable.)

24 CAROB

A carat is not a measure of size, but of weight. Long ago, Arab traders used carob seeds, which are small and uniformly-sized, to weigh jewels on balance scales. A single carob seed weighs about one-fifth of a gram so a 5-carat diamond weighs one gram.

WHAT KIND OF WATCHES ARE AVAILABLE?

The selection of men's and women's watches usually includes well-known brands across a wide range of prices, styles, and movements (i.e., mechanical, quartz, or digital). There are rugged sports watches like Hublot, Tag Heuer, and Invicta; dress watches like Mont Blanc, Raymond Weil, Omega, IWC, Rolex, and Harry Winston; and high-quality everyday watches like Seiko and Timex. Smart watches like Apple, Samsung, and Fitbit devices are usually displayed separately in the digital electronics area of the warehouse. Prices range from several hundred dollars for a Timex to almost $30,000 for an Omega.

KIRKLAND SIGNATURE

IN 2022, COSTCO SOLD
OVER $58 BILLION IN
KS PRODUCTS — ABOUT 25%
OF ALL REVENUES
(EXCLUDING GASOLINE)

WHAT'S THE HISTORY OF COSTCO'S KIRKLAND SIGNATURE PRIVATE LABEL BRAND?

In the early years, Costco used different brand names for various products — Simply Soda, Clout Detergent, Nutra Nuggets Dog Food — which Jim Sinegal later described as "forgettable." By the early 1990s, Jim felt that pricing increases for brand name products "created an umbrella" under which Costco could launch a unified private label brand. In 1995, further encouraged by high-quality private label activity in the UK (e.g., Marks & Spencer, Sainsbury), Jim, with Jeff Brotman, launched Kirkland Signature, a line of private label goods as good as or better than national brands, at lower prices. Consolidating under one brand name would build loyalty, reduce consumer confusion, and save money on legal fees for trademarking.

HOW LARGE IS COSTCO'S KIRKLAND SIGNATURE BUSINESS?

As of 2022, there were over 1,000 items with the Kirkland Signature brand name and sales were greater than Campbell's Soup, Kellogg's, and Hershey brands *combined*. Two of Costco's top-selling KS products — bath tissue and paper towels — each generate over $1 billion in sales annually. The first KS product was vitamins, which was an immediate success. Now, everything from nuts to paper products, from wine to hot dogs — even golf balls — are offered under the Kirkland Signature brand.

HOW WAS THE KIRKLAND SIGNATURE BRAND NAME SELECTED?

Management initially wanted to use "Seattle Signature," but that name was unavailable. Costco was originally headquartered in the Seattle suburb of Kirkland, so they used "Kirkland Signature." Bob Craves, a founding officer, sketched the logo on a napkin at dinner one evening with Jim Sinegal. When the company later moved to nearby Issaquah, they decided not to change the name — in part because it's more difficult to spell!

WHO MANUFACTURES KIRKLAND SIGNATURE ITEMS?

It's no secret that Duracell, Huggies, and Reynolds Wrap all produce Kirkland Signature items that compete head-to-head at Costco with their own national brands. Bumble Bee produces Costco's albacore tuna under the KS label. KS mattresses are made by Stearns and Foster. It is simply urban myth that KS French Vodka is made by Grey Goose — although at one time the two brands shared a water source. Costco will occasionally co-brand KS with another name brand, especially when the other brand is iconic, such as Jelly Belly jelly beans.

BOB CRAVES

In 1983, founding officer Bob Craves was working as a marketing executive at Builders Emporium in Los Angeles when Jim Sinegal recruited his former colleague to join Costco as head of membership and marketing. In 2000, Bob retired and co-founded the College Success Foundation, providing college scholarships and mentoring to low-income youth. In 2014, after Bob passed away at age 72, Jim told the *Los Angeles Times* "Bob could always find the good thing in every situation. Most people couldn't."

K

TOP 5 BEST-SELLING KIRKLAND SIGNATURE ITEMS in 2022:

1. **BATH TISSUE**
$1.4 BILLION

2. **PAPER TOWELS**
$1.2 BILLION

3. **BOTTLED WATER**
$730 MILLION

4. **DIAPERS**
$650 MILLION

5. **LARGE EGGS**
$498 MILLION

ARE ALL KIRKLAND SIGNATURE ITEMS SUCCESSFUL?

Costco is as commercially disciplined with KS products as they are with anything else. KS items never sell for more than 15% above cost and are rigorously quality-tested. Costco warehouse real estate is valuable: if a product doesn't sell, it's pulled regardless of the brand name. KS toothpaste couldn't compete with Colgate and Crest, so it was discontinued. For some time, Costco sold Kirkland Signature Mac & Cheese to compete with Kraft. It didn't fail, *per se*, but Costco discontinued the item after concluding that it wasn't possible to make a *better* product at a *lower* price.

KOSHER

KIRKLAND SIGNATURE BRAND INCLUDES OVER 900 KOSHER PRODUCTS

WHAT IS KOSHER FOOD?

The Hebrew word "kosher" means "fit," i.e., food that is kosher is fit to eat, according to the Jewish religion's sacred texts and commentary from the past two thousand years. Too complex to summarize here, some rules may be familiar even to non-Jews: no pork, no shellfish, and no mixing of dairy and meat dishes. The standards are exacting: they run the gamut from the proper slaughtering method for animals to the manufacturing of wine. Kosher foods bear a mark — known as a "hechsher" — on the packaging.

DOES COSTCO SELL KOSHER FOOD OUTSIDE THE US OR ONLINE?

Costco in Canada and Mexico have substantial kosher selections, particularly in Montréal and Mexico City. Outside of North America, the selection is more restricted. The Costco website has a page titled "Kosher Kirkland Signature Grocery," which lists kosher foods. There is an active Facebook page called "Kosher Costco" which has 56,000 members and is another good resource.

WHAT KINDS OF KOSHER FOOD ARE SOLD AT A TYPICAL COSTCO?

Costco food buyers will invariably opt for the kosher option when choosing between two similar items. Kosher food can be expensive, so members who "keep kosher" appreciate the quality and pricing of Costco's kosher products. Many national brands, like Kellogg's, Hershey, and Chobani have kosher certification, as do popular brands like Skinny Pop and Pirate's Booty in the snack aisles. While prepared Deli items are generally not kosher, some items in the Deli coolers are kosher and some warehouses even have separate kosher Deli coolers. Fresh fruit and vegetables generally do not require kosher certification.

SIMCHA!

In the US, the kosher market is $22 billion and growing at about 4% a year.

First launched in the 1990s, there are now 23 kosher Costco Bakeries in the US, mainly near Miami and New York City.

K

DOES EVERY WAREHOUSE CARRY KOSHER ITEMS?

Yes, but in regions with higher concentrations of Jewish families, like New York City, Chicago, Miami, and Los Angeles, there will be a greater selection and perhaps even fresh packaged kosher meat and chicken. Costco also operates kosher Bakeries in select warehouses, which are inspected on a regular basis by licensed professionals to certify that the facility is kosher. Two Costco warehouses with significant kosher sections are in Lawrence, New York — about 15 miles southeast of Manhattan — and Miami.

LINGO

HOW TO SPEAK "COSTCO" — HELPFUL TERMS & EXPRESSIONS

ANCILLARY BUSINESSES:
Warehouse departments, including Gasoline, Optical, Pharmacy, Food Court, Hearing Aids, and Tire Service Center.

BACK-HAUL:
Truckload picked up at a vendor and delivered to the Costco depot on the return trip from the warehouse to the depot, after dropping off merchandise.

BLOCK DOWN:
To clean, square, and level off a pallet of merchandise.

BOX RUN (OR DE-BOXING):
Moving empty boxes from the sales floor to the front end to pack purchases.

DEATH STAR:
A colloquial term used by members to refer to the asterisk in the upper-right corner of an item's price tag which means the item may be discontinued. For some members, this is a prompt to stock up on a favorite product that might soon be gone for a brief rest or forever.

DEPOTS:
Costco's distribution centers.

DOMESTICS:
Warehouse departments for bedding — sheets, blankets, pillows — and towels.

DNI:
An acronym for Do Not Inventory. Refers to merchandise which is not inventoried because it is discontinued and is **RTV**.

DOOR COUNT:
The number of members who enter the warehouse in a given period. The average door count for a warehouse is 3,500 per day.

DRY SIDE:
The depot area for unrefrigerated items.

FEFO:
An acronym for First Expired First Out. The way merchandise is rotated to ensure freshness.

FRESH FOODS:
Warehouse departments that include Bakery, Deli, Fish, Meat, and Produce.

FRESHEN AT FIVE:
Tidying and replenishing the warehouse at around 5 PM to make sure it is **Showtime Ready** even during the final hours of business. Different warehouses may have different terms for this, but the practice is universal.

GENTLE SWEEP:
At the end of the day, a group of employees walks through the warehouse with a friendly warning for members that closing time is approaching . Also referred to as a gentle push.

L

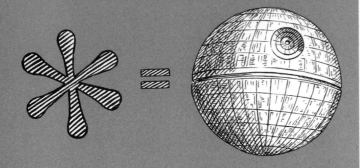

KIOSK:
On the walk to the warehouse exit, near the Membership Counter, are Costco displays offering services like HVAC, kitchen design, insurance, auto sales, and even caskets. [SEE "CASKETS"] Kiosk also refers to the self-service ordering terminals at the Food Court.

MAJORS:
The warehouse department selling computers, TVs, and electronics, it is staffed by employees usually wearing red vests, readily available to answer technical questions.

PANDA WATCH:
The state of alert after being informed of an impending senior management **Store Check** and also the phrase used by zoo staff awaiting the birth of a baby panda. Rumor has it that some airport personnel alert local warehouses that the corporate jet has landed, aka **The Eagle Has Landed.**

PRICING:
When a price has a ".97" at the end, it means the item has been marked down by a supplier; a price ending with ".00" refers to a warehouse markdown.

PULLING WEEDS:
Relocating warehouse merchandise that is not in its proper home or removing actual weeds in the parking lot.

GO-BACKS:
Items a member has decided, at checkout, not to purchase. Those items are usually gathered in carts near the front end. An employee tasked with returning this merchandise to its proper location is said to be "doing go-backs".

GREEN INK:
Co-founder Jim Sinegal's preferred color, even used to sign documents approving new warehouse locations. Within Costco, this term may be used as either a noun or a verb. Examples: "We've gone to green ink for the new warehouse," or "The Costco site on Mars has been green-inked."

HABA:
An acronym for another warehouse department, Health And Beauty Aids, usually located adjacent to the Pharmacy.

HARDLINES:
Non-food warehouse departments that include HABA, office products, automotive, hardware, major appliances, sporting goods, toys, garden, and patio.

RACETRACK:

The typical path from the warehouse entrance, past **Hardlines, Softlines,** and **Fresh Foods** to the rear of the store, then looping back to the front-end registers along the other side of the warehouse. The rotisserie chicken is usually at the far end of this configuration.

RETURN TO VENDOR (RTV):

Unsold or defective items that are returned to the supplier for credit. These items are returned to the depot and, depending on the vendor's policy, are often donated rather than returned to vendor.

ROADSHOW:

Special merchandise displayed in the warehouse for a limited time (e.g., handbags, blenders, massage chairs, BBQ grills), often with a demonstration and always with a vendor representative to answer questions.

SHOWTIME READY:

Everything in order — clean, neat, and straight — and ready for business, like a Broadway show about to open.

SOFTLINES:

The warehouse section that contains apparel, domestics, housewares, small electrics, jewelry, books, media, and furniture.

STEEL:

The shelving above the merchandise where additional product inventory is stored. "Up in the steel" is the most common use of this term. Walking through the aisles every hour on the hour to ensure things are neat and tidy — no trash or spills or other issues that need attention — is known as a "steel walk."

STOCK KEEPING UNIT (SKU):

An SKU refers to an individual item of sale, marked by a bar code that identifies it at checkout. Costco is vigilant about never carrying more than 3,800 SKU's (pronounced "skews").

STORE CHECK:

A visit to a Costco warehouse by any level of management, typically unannounced. **(See Panda Watch** and **The Eagle Has Landed)** Jim Sinegal famously visited every warehouse at least once each year until the numbers became so large it was no longer possible. Senior management carries on this tradition as best they can, visiting each existing warehouse every 18-24 months, and attending every new warehouse opening.

SUNDRIES:

The warehouse area that contains bath tissue, paper towels, pet food, laundry detergent, dishwashing, wraps, and beverages.

THE EAGLE HAS LANDED:

The Costco employees checking membership cards at the front entrance may announce over the walkie talkie that "the Eagle has landed" or "we have a visitor." (See **Panda Watch**)

THE FENCE:

Mesh fencing at every warehouse, just inside the front door, used to display seasonal merchandise or promotional items, often on sale. This term harkens back to the first Price Club warehouse, in San Diego (now Costco warehouse #401), which had a floor-to-ceiling fence in its entryway. Rather than spend money to remove this intrusive artifact of the building's previous use, Rick Libenson, then Head of Merchandising for Price Club, pragmatically decided to use it for merchandising.

TRADE AREA:

The distance Costco members will travel to visit a warehouse.

TREASURE HUNT:

The shopping experience at Costco, which often involves looking for **"Wow"** Items — seasonal or unique merchandise that may prompt an impulse purchase.

UPC (UNIVERSAL PRODUCT CODE):

The bar code on an item scanned at checkout for pricing information.

WET SIDE:

The depot designation for refrigerated and frozen foods.

"WOW" ITEM:

You'll know one when you see one! The 2022 Winter Glitter Globe is one of our favorite examples: a light-up snow globe filled with gin-liqueur and edible gold flakes, which sold for only $19.99. (See **Treasure Hunt**)

LOGISTICS

COSTCO'S EFFICIENT
LOGISTICS SYSTEM IS KEY TO
KEEPING PRICES LOW

HOW BIG IS COSTCO'S DEPOT SYSTEM?

In May 1988, Jim Sinegal and Dick DiCerchio were disappointed with the operations at a third-party depot they visited in Los Angeles, so they asked Tom Walker — already in charge of warehouse construction — to create a proprietary depot system for Costco. Moving this function in-house resulted in an immediate 5% savings that have only increased since. As of March 2023, Costco had 26 depots, totaling more than 30 million square feet, which serve as distribution hubs. The depots are located around the world: 15 in the US, four in Canada, two in Japan, and one each in Australia, Mexico, South Korea, Taiwan, and the UK. A single depot may serve anywhere from 20 to 80 warehouses in its area — the average is about 45 warehouses. The largest depot is in Mira Loma, California.

WHAT IS NET LANDED COST?

One of the key ingredients in Costco's secret sauce is a laser focus on "net landed cost" — the cost of bringing a product from manufacturer to the warehouse shelves. While Costco turns its inventory much more frequently than other retailers (eleven times each year), individual items are handled as infrequently as possible. Typical supermarkets unpack products and stock shelves by hand; Costco's products remain largely on pallets, moving from the dock to "the steel" **[SEE "LINGO"]** without being handled by employees. Often, the first time a Costco employee touches an individual item is at the front-end registers. All of this helps keep costs down — and prices, too.

IS THERE ANYTHING UNIQUE ABOUT COSTCO'S TRUCKING OPERATION?

Costco has a fleet of some 5,300 trailers and 700 tractors, along with 1,600 drivers. All the vehicles are monitored in real time by individual depot control systems that track fuel usage and other issues. Safety is paramount: drivers are not allowed on the road in dangerous weather or other hazardous situations. The drivers use a checklist system to ensure the trucks are road-worthy, checking tire pressure, fluid levels, brake lights, and turn signals. Costco fleet drivers do not handle long-haul assignments; if the destination is outside a 220-mile radius of the depot, third-party long-haul shippers deliver the load. If they want to, Costco's truck drivers can sleep at home every night.

HOW DOES PRODUCT GET FROM THE DEPOT TO THE WAREHOUSE SHELF?

After inbound product arrives at the depot, it is checked by Quality Assurance. If accepted, it remains on pallets and is moved with forklifts to the outbound docks, where it is loaded onto trucks and sent to the warehouses. At the warehouse, all products are logged in and processed: dry (unrefrigerated) items are loaded onto the sales floor between 4 AM and warehouse opening; fresh, refrigerated items go to the sales floor immediately, throughout the day.

"WET" DEPOTS HANDLE FRESH AND FROZEN FOODS; "DRY" BUILDINGS HANDLE EVERYTHING ELSE

WHAT IS A BACK-HAUL?

Truck drivers might return to the depot with items from the warehouse: stuff returned by members, empty pallets, or bales of compacted cardboard, in what is called a "back-haul" of inventory. Drivers might also pick up a shipment from a local vendor's warehouse. Costco's trucks are well-utilized and rarely travel empty. Each truck makes an average of two "turns" a day, i.e., trips from depot to warehouse and back.

IT TAKES ONLY SIX DAYS FOR COSTCO'S FRESH-CUT ROSES TO TRAVEL FROM SOUTH AMERICAN FARMS TO US WAREHOUSES

HOW ARE E-COMMERCE ORDERS AND RETURNS HANDLED?

Standard depots handle some online orders, but the bulk of these operations in the US are processed by two very large depots dedicated to e-commerce — in Mira Loma, California and Frederick, Maryland. Returned items are either destroyed, returned to the vendor, or donated to World Vision, a not-for-profit that supports communities in need.
[SEE "GOOD WORKS"]

HOW DID COSTCO DEAL WITH THE SHIPPING LOGJAM THAT STARTED IN 2020?

Offshore warehouses, like those in Hawaii, Alaska, Iceland, and Sweden, are supplied by ship. In the past, Costco's shipping has been done by third-party shipping companies like Matson. However, during the pandemic, the logistics crunch at major ports throughout the world prompted Costco to lease seven vessels and containers, as well. The leased vessels handle smaller loads than standard fleets (800-1500 containers versus 10,000 on a standard vessel), which allows vessels to be unloaded in several hours instead of three to four days.

WHAT IS INNOVEL?

In March 2020, after five years of working together, Costco purchased Innovel Solutions, an Illinois-based logistics company, from Sears' holding company for $1 billion. Innovel covers the US and Puerto Rico, specializing in final-mile delivery, installation of large appliances, and white-glove services. It is especially useful for large and bulky deliveries (furniture and major appliances). The purchase included 11 regional distribution centers, 104 market delivery options, three call centers, and 15 million square feet of warehouse space.

WHAT IS CROSS-DOCKING?

First used in the trucking industry in the 1930s, and by the US military in the 1950s, cross-docking is a system in which inbound trucks carrying goods arrive at receiving docks on one side of a depot; the goods are then loaded into outbound trucks on the other side. In 1994, following the Costco/Price Club merger, Tom Walker introduced cross-docking to Costco. Depot employees move incoming pallets from the receiving side across to the shipping side and, on the same day, load them onto trucks headed to warehouses, usually leaving the depots empty overnight, thereby reducing inventory holding costs.

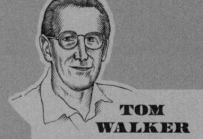

TOM WALKER

Born and raised in Houston, Tom served in the US Air Force for four years after high school. In 1963, he got an entry level job at FedMart in Houston and remained with the company for 18 years, becoming VP, Distribution. In July 1983, Tom joined Costco as a founding officer, and helped start the company. He was hired to open and run the second warehouse (Portland). In May 1984, Tom launched the Florida division and within the year was promoted to VP, SE Operations. Over the next 21 years, Tom oversaw construction, distribution, traffic, facilities, purchasing, and the flight department until his retirement in 2013.

L

MAJORS

COSTCO'S
TOP SELLING NON-FOODS
DEPARTMENT

WHAT THE HECK ARE "MAJORS"?

Majors is Costco lingo for major electronics and appliances. It covers everything you normally see as you enter a warehouse: TVs, computers, and floor-standing appliances like refrigerators, washing machines, and dryers. Costco sells these products worldwide, in compliance with local technical standards for voltage and frequency.

WHAT KIND OF SERVICE DOES COSTCO PROVIDE FOR MAJORS?

Majors is the only department that usually has a staff member on hand to answer questions. These employees are familiar with product specs and industry trends, and may even suggest waiting to buy if a newer item is about to be released. In the US and Canada, in addition to the electronics manufacturer's one-year warranty from date of purchase, Costco offers members a free one-year extension on their warranty. In the US, Canada, and the UK, Costco also offers a telephone "concierge service," which is a helpline that provides technical support for electronic products bought at Costco. The idea for this came from CEO Craig Jelinek, when Costco realized that so-called "smart" TVs were sufficiently complicated that members would benefit from help when they brought the product home.

WHY ARE THEY ALWAYS NEAR THE FRONT DOOR?

In the 1950s, Majors was one of the few non-concession departments in the original FedMart store, so Leo Freedman, then FedMart's president, placed it near the front door to drive sales. Later on, FedMart moved Majors towards the back of the store, but Price Club usually kept them near the entrance, to showcase the fast-paced innovations in color TVs pioneered by Sony and others. At Costco today, large flat screen TVs present a riot of attention-getting color at the front entrance, along with an ever-changing variety of laptops, tablets, and gaming computers for customers eager to discover the latest in digital media.

MEAT

IN 2019, COSTCO'S TWO MEAT PROCESSING PLANTS PRODUCED 244 MILLION POUNDS OF MEAT

HOW DOES MEAT GET TO THE COSTCO WAREHOUSE?

Some meat goes directly from suppliers to warehouses via depots, and some meat goes to one of Costco's two meat processing facilities, near Stockton, California and Chicago. At the processing plants, the meat is ground and packed into "chubs" — cylindrical plastic packs — or formed into patties, meatballs, hot dogs, and organic beef "bricks." [SEE "HOT DOGS" AND "COSTCO WHOLESALE INDUSTRIES"] The two processing plants are co-located with Costco depots; meat from those depots is distributed to warehouses around the world. [SEE "LOGISTICS"]

WHEN DID COSTCO START SELLING FRESH MEAT?

In 1987, Costco — led by Stan McMurray and Tim Rose, two of the founding officers with extensive grocery experience — began selling fresh foods. Fresh meat is a particular challenge, given the importance of food safety, but over the years Costco has become one of the country's leading purveyors of USDA Prime and Choice beef. Some warehouses occasionally sell exotic products like ground bison; boar and elk meat can be found in Canada at times; and Alaska often sells reindeer sausage.

HOW IS THE MEAT SOURCED?

Domestic US beef comes from a handful of family ranches in California. Almost all the pork comes from the JB Swift company. Lamb is sourced from Australia, but with Costco's 2022 opening in New Zealand, that country's famous lamb may also start appearing in warehouses. Poultry comes from Costco's Nebraska poultry facility or local suppliers. Overseas, many countries have rules and regulations that limit imported meat, so you may find only local meat. However, USDA Prime and Choice are quite popular in Asian warehouses. [SEE "CHICKEN"]

HOW DOES COSTCO MAINTAIN FOOD SAFETY IN THE MEAT DEPARTMENT?

Sanitation specialists work in every Meat department to ensure that the meat is safely prepared and safe to eat. Meat is tested frequently for bacteria and impurities, and inspected to ensure that it complies with labelling standards. The USDA regularly inspects Costco warehouses and has an inspection team permanently stationed at Costco's two meat processing facilities. Testing is only part of the safety routine. Every evening, in a process that takes up to three hours, sanitation specialists take every piece of equipment apart and clean it thoroughly with disinfectant, so that the next morning the butchers who come to work know that they are using sterile equipment.

WHY DID COSTCO OPEN ITS OWN MEAT PROCESSING FACILITIES?

These facilities allow Costco to control quality and safety, and to reduce costs. For example, in 1997, suppliers were charging Costco $2.30-$2.50 per pound for meatballs. It took two years, but Costco began producing their own KS meatballs at one of their meat processing plants for about 40% less. By 2009, Costco was producing some 14 million pounds of tastier, cheaper meatballs — at about 6,000 pounds per hour!

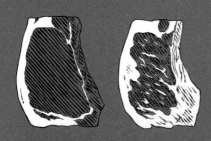

USDA MEAT GRADINGS

are based on the amount and distribution of fat within meat. More evenly marbled cuts are Prime; Choice has less fat or is not as evenly marbled.

MEMBERS

IN 2006, COSTCO OPENED
A WAREHOUSE IN
GYPSUM, COLORADO, A TOWN
NEAR VAIL AND ASPEN
WITH A MAJESTIC BACKDROP,
BUT A POPULATION OF
ONLY 5,000 PEOPLE!

HOW MANY MEMBERS DOES COSTCO HAVE WORLDWIDE?

As of February 12, 2023, Costco had 123 million cardholders worldwide, representing over 68 million households. For the past ten years, the annual growth rate has been over 6%. Recently, much of that growth has occurred overseas as Costco has expanded in Asia and Europe. A large part of Costco's success is the consistently high member-renewal rate — an impressive 90%.

WHAT IS THE DEMOGRAPHIC OF THE TYPICAL COSTCO MEMBER?

Costco estimates that a typical US member is around 54 years old with an annual household income above $100,000. (On average, only 22% of all US shoppers have household incomes above $100,000.) Costco draws its shoppers from predominantly urban or suburban settings, as opposed to some of its competitors who are more rural-based.

HOW DOES COSTCO MEMBERSHIP BREAK DOWN GEOGRAPHICALLY AND BY TYPE?

The majority of members live in North America; the Asia/Australia/New Zealand region has the second-largest number of members; Europe is the smallest region but is expected to grow as Costco expands in France, Spain, and Sweden. About 80% of Costco shoppers are basic Gold Star members, the rest are Business members. Executive Gold Star members and Executive Business members pay more for membership, but get rebates and special deals. They represent about 55% of the US and Canada membership, and about 17% of the membership in Mexico, the UK, Japan, South Korea, and Taiwan.

ANY EXAMPLES OF HOW DEVOTED COSTCO FANS ARE?

Not all Costco members are as devoted as yours truly, driven to write and self-publish a fan book, but we do have good company. There are many other Costco members who are passionate about the retailer. Here are a few real-life examples of true dedication:

PROPOSALS AND WEDDINGS
AT COSTCO WAREHOUSES

HALLOWEEN COSTUMES
— NOT JUST THOSE BOUGHT AT COSTCO: ACTUALLY DRESSING UP
AS A COSTCO EMPLOYEE OR EVEN AS A HOT DOG

COSTCO ROAD TRIPS
(SEE "YONKERS TO YORBA LINDA")

A COLLEGE APPLICATION ABOUT COSTCO HELPED ONE YOUNG WOMAN
GAIN ADMISSION TO FIVE IVY LEAGUE SCHOOLS

A GROUP OF VETERANS GATHER WEEKLY AT
THE BRENTWOOD, TENNESSEE COSTCO FOOD COURT

"COSTCO PRODUCTS AND REVIEWS" FACEBOOK PAGE
WITH OVER 500,000 MEMBERS

"COSTCOHOTFINDS" ON TIKTOK
HAS OVER ONE MILLION FOLLOWERS

WHAT ARE THE PERKS OF BEING AN EXECUTIVE MEMBER?

In 1997, Costco introduced the Executive Membership Program, a plan to reward high-volume members with cash rebates and other perks. Initially the program had five benefits, including personal and business check printing at a considerable discount from what most banks charged. Although all members in the US and Puerto Rico can purchase checks through Costco, Executive members receive an extra 20% in savings. By 2007, the Executive Membership Program offered members 20 different services.

JOE PORTERA

Joe worked at FedMart and several other retailers before he was lured by a 35% *pay cut* to join Costco in March 1984 as general manager of the Portland, Oregon warehouse. By the end of 1984, Joe was promoted to VP/ROM and moved to Canada to help with Costco's expansion. In 1986, he moved to the Bay Area as VP and regional manager. In 1991, he was promoted to SVP/Non-Foods Buying at the Seattle Home Office. He returned to the Bay Area briefly in 1994 before his promotion (and another move) to EVP/COO Eastern division; in 2002, the Canada division was added to his responsibilities. In 2010, Joe became the second Chief Diversity Officer.

He retired in 2022.

DOES COSTCO HAVE ANY CELEBRITY MEMBERS?

Yes, of course! Keep your eyes peeled!

SHOWTIME

MERCHANDISING

> COSTCO WAREHOUSES
> ARE "SHOWTIME READY"
> ALL DAY LONG

WHAT IS MERCHANDISING?

Merchandising is the presentation and promotion of products in either a retail or wholesale setting. Costco combines the two with stunning results: a large no-frills warehouse with meticulously displayed products still on shipping pallets in a faux-industrial environment. Look around and you might see a fully assembled playhouse high above the shelves, a mountain of Spam cans piled artfully at the end of an aisle, or an air hockey table that you can test out. The Bakery, Deli, and Meat department employees work as if on a stage, so Costco members can watch behind the scenes while shopping. In Mexico, behold the mini-donut machine or in Japan, marvel at the sushi conveyor belt. This is more than shopping — it's a Treasure Hunt with free samples!

WHAT ARE THE SIX RIGHTS OF MERCHANDISING?

In the 1950s, Sol Price pioneered the Six Rights of Merchandising: the right product in the right place at the right time in the right quantity and right condition at the right price. It takes considerable discipline to limit the number of items sold across a wide range of product categories, offering high-quality goods for very low prices, but Costco remains true to this strategy in every one of more than 850 warehouses around the world. Products are carefully selected and sold "early in early out": for example, Costco has finished selling Halloween candy before many retailers even start to sell it. Produce that is starting to fade is pulled from the shelves and donated. **[SEE "GOOD WORKS"]** Everything at Costco is vetted with three basic questions: Can we do it well? Can we save members money? Can we make a bit of profit?

WHAT IS A ROADSHOW?

From time to time, a warehouse will sponsor a Roadshow **[SEE "LINGO"]** featuring special merchandise sold directly by the vendor inside a Costco warehouse. In 2017, select California warehouses offered two different model Bösendorfer pianos for a 20% savings. We were awed by a Roadshow in Japan selling whole fresh salmon *and* salmon roe, all displayed on ice in the Fish department. In Seoul, we saw several Roadshows with both men's and women's high-end clothing. Roadshows typically last seven to ten days and can appear in any part of the warehouse.

WHAT DOES IT MEAN TO BE "SHOWTIME READY"?

The highest compliment you can give a Costco employee is to say that something looks "showtime ready," as if the curtain was about to go up on a performance. At 4 AM every morning, Costco employees arrive, the loading dock crew begins receiving merchandise, manned forklifts ferry pallets of product around, end-aisle displays are created, and the shelves are restocked. Throughout the day, employees continuously restock and freshen product displays and tidy the sales floor — especially apparel, which is always at risk of looking tousled as some 3,500 members pass through the warehouse on an average day, many stopping to search for a particular size of a must-have clothing item.

PLAY IT AGAIN, RON

As Ron Vachris, then EVP/COO, Merchandising, observed: "Only at Costco can you come in to pick up a prescription and leave with a $100,000 piano!"

WHAT IS THE TREASURE HUNT?

The Treasure Hunt begins at the Seattle Home Office or regional offices, where Costco's buyers search for products that will tickle the fancy of discriminating consumers and culminates in the warehouses, as members walk up and down the aisles, on the alert for great finds at great prices. It's hard to imagine that anyone goes to Costco expecting to find truffle carpaccio or dill pickle-flavored cashews, but turn a corner and you may find these items or other treasures, all top quality and well-priced. In the Business Centers, merchandise doesn't get moved around as frequently, but in regular Costco warehouses, items are often moved to showcase the latest arrivals or special deals and to keep things exciting.

WHAT IS THE FENCE?

The merchandise on display along the fence that separates the entrance and the exit is another one of Costco's merchandising techniques. As the seasons change, so do the products along the fence, with back to school items in August, and vitamins and other healthy choices in January to assist with New Year's resolutions. Products along the fence are very often specially priced or in limited supply, sometimes promoted by a vendor. The fence "schedule" is jointly developed by the Home Office and regional merchandising teams, with flexibility for input from any warehouse general manager. At Costco, everyone is involved in merchandising.

IN 2022, MEXICO RANKED THIRD FOR NUMBER OF WAREHOUSES PER COUNTRY, AFTER ONLY THE US AND CANADA

MEXICO

WHAT PROMPTED COSTCO TO EXPAND INTO MEXICO?

In the early 1990s, the US was negotiating the North American Free Trade Agreement (NAFTA) with Mexico and Canada. Anticipating a dramatic reduction of trade barriers, Costco and Price Club, competitors at the time, each began to explore opportunities for expansion into Mexico. Costco was in discussions with Gigante, a retail conglomerate run by the Losada family, and Price Club with Controladora Commercial Mexicana (CCM), a retail conglomerate controlled by the Gonzalez family. Price Club's negotiations concluded more quickly, and their first Mexican warehouse opened on Leap Day, February 29, 1992, in Satélite, a suburb of Mexico City. In early 1993, Costco ended their discussions with Gigante when merger negotiations with Price Club began: the newly merged company moved forward with CCM.

HOW BIG IS COSTCO'S MEXICAN BUSINESS?

Boosted by the removal of trade barriers, Mexico soon had 11 Costco warehouses. However, in March 1994, the country entered a prolonged financial downturn; only two new warehouses were opened over the next four years. Fortunately, in 1998 the economy stabilized and Costco resumed its steady growth, opening an additional 28 warehouses by 2022. Costco in Mexico now has over 1.5 million members, with five warehouses in Mexico City alone, and is considered part of the San Diego region.

DOES COSTCO STILL HAVE A BUSINESS PARTNER IN MEXICO?

Costco senior executives consider the partnership with CCM to be one of the most successful of the international partnerships. However, in the wake of the 2008 financial crisis, CCM sold their 50% stake back to Costco for 10.7 billion pesos ($767 million). While this particular alliance was fruitful, Costco prefers not to have a partner; generally, many partners want to increase prices, which is anathema to Costco.

UNIQUE MEXICAN COSTCO ITEMS:

MOLE CHICKEN CROISSANT SANDWICHES

PAELLA SOLD NEXT TO ROTISSERIE CHICKEN (WEEKENDS ONLY)

JALAPEÑO PEPPER DISPENSER AT THE FOOD COURT

ARE THERE ANY DIFFERENCES IN THE BAKERY?

The big attraction in the Bakery — unique to Mexico — is the deep fryer/conveyor belt setup used to make mini donuts, which are then hand-rolled in cinnamon sugar and packed 30 to a box. Chocolate was invented in Mexico thousands of years ago and Mexicans still love it. Choc-oholics will delight in the mini-chocolate fudge cakes with chocolate icing and the "brownie cake," a light brownie-based cake with chocolate chunks and choco-late icing. Croissants are filled with strawberries and dusted with sugar. **[SEE "XALAPA" FOR OTHER MEXICAN BAKERY ITEMS]**

WHAT IS SPECIAL ABOUT THE SANTA FE WAREHOUSE?

Built in November, 2021, the warehouse is unique in design and location, situated on the edge of a natural gorge overlooking the magnificent 69-acre Parque La Mexicana, in a modern business district west of Mexico City. While Costco traditionally purchases the land for warehouses, this extraordinary location is leased. On the warehouse roof there's a soccer field, tennis and paddle ball courts, a contemplative garden, and a skateboard park, all open to the public free of charge! The cost of this unusual rooftop was about half the cost of the entire project, and is an example of the way in which Costco gives back to a community.

M

WHAT IS UNUSUAL ABOUT THE PARKING LOTS IN MEXICO?

The Mexican Costco parking lots are manned by men in white shirts with black pants who help customers to their cars with their purchases, but the men are not employed by Costco. They also return the carts to the warehouse, which is normally a Costco employee's responsibility.

WHAT ARE SOME UNIQUE FOOD ITEMS AT MEXICAN WAREHOUSES?

The fresh food at the Mexican warehouses is truly distinctive, with tuna pie, smoked salmon focaccia sandwiches, and packaged smoked fish (mackerel, tuna, and salmon) in the Deli section. Costco sells nopal — prickly pear cactus pads — in many forms: large bags of fresh organic nopal in the produce section; refrigerated packages of panela cheese with nopal in some regions; and nopal churritos (crispy, savory corn-and-nopal snack bits) in the snack section. There's a large selection of salsas and hot sauces displayed with a wide variety of tortillas, olives, beans, rice, and many varieties of canned jalapeños. Imported goods are shipped from the Costco depot in Houston, Texas.

NEW ZEALAND

WITHIN THE FIRST SIX MONTHS, OVER 150,000 NEW MEMBERS SIGNED UP AT NEW ZEALAND'S FIRST COSTCO WAREHOUSE

ISN'T NEW ZEALAND JUST AN ISLAND OFF THE COAST OF AUSTRALIA?

Not on your life! New Zealand, a remote nation consisting of two main islands and about 600 smaller ones, is 1,000 miles southeast of Sydney. Australia and New Zealand are both fully independent members of the British Commonwealth. With a distinctive Māori-influenced history and culture, New Zealand is thought to be the last major land mass inhabited by humans, dating from the early 1300s when Polynesian explorers first arrived.

WHEN DID COSTCO COME ASHORE?

On September 28, 2022, Costco opened its first New Zealand warehouse, in Westgate, just outside of Auckland, the country's largest city and home to the largest Polynesian population in the world. Similar to Iceland, Costco's high-value/low-price proposition was welcomed in this remote country heavily dependent on high-priced imported goods. New Zealanders are known as "kiwis," after their national bird, which is flightless because it lacked mammalian predators. New Zealand's total population is just over 5 million, about one-third of whom live in Auckland. Kiwis – the human variety – showed up *en masse* for Costco's opening day. The warehouse sold out of hot dogs before noon, and Costco contracted with a nearby garage to provide parking for more than 500 cars. As of March 2023, Costco is considering a second warehouse in New Zealand.

[SEE "AUSTRALIA" AND "ICELAND"]

KIWIS EVERYWHERE!

KIWI FRUIT are native to China, but were first commercially produced in New Zealand in the early 20th century.

KIWI BIRDS are endemic to New Zealand and national icons.

Guess what? New Zealanders are also known as KIWIS!

ANY NOTEWORTHY NON-FOOD ITEMS IN NEW ZEALND?

Since much of the non-food buying is done by Australian buyers, there are a lot of items that are popular in Australia, too. For example, Kiwis are as enamored of barbecue as their neighbors to the northwest, and so barbecues, wood chips, and other grilling gear are readily available, as well as a wood-fired pizza oven for about $3,000 US. Kiwis are sporty, so Costco offers a range of bikes and scooters, Cobra and Kirkland Signature golfing gear, tennis rackets, skateboards, exercise equipment, a basketball hoop, air hockey table, and other similar items.

WHAT ARE SOME DIFFERENCES FROM OTHER COSTCOS?

The first noticeable difference is that department signage is in both English and Māori, the country's two official written languages. Māori is spoken by the indigenous people of New Zealand, who comprise about 17% of the population. Products are generally similar to the US, although much of the inventory is sourced either from New Zealand or Australia, where the regional buying office is located. The exterior design of the Westgate warehouse is stylish, black and white and modern. Unlike Asia's multi-story shopping levels, it's a 150,000 square foot single shopping floor, with three parking levels above it containing some 800 parking spaces.

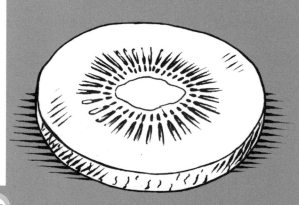

IS THE FRESH FOOD LOCAL?

Kiwis are justifiably proud of their produce, especially tangy/sweet lemonade apples, red kumara (a kind of sweet potato), fejoias (pineapple guavas), and a ruby red variety of their eponymous furry fruit commercialized in 2022. In the Bakery, notable items are cheesecakes, with either lemon/passion fruit or salted caramel toppings, and a package of "slices," cookie bars in a variety of flavors. For Anzac Day on April 25th, a day of national remembrance, New Zealand (and Australia) both offer Anzac biscuits, oatmeal/coconut cookies. Meat highlights are New Zealand lamb, local wagyu beef, and fresh whole quail and duck. Locally caught whole fish like Marlborough Sounds King Salmon or Trevally, a delicious, meaty seawater fish, are offered alongside prawns (cooked and raw), John Dory fillets, and wild abalone. The Deli section has many of the same items you'd find elsewhere, such as chicken street taco kits, macaroni and cheese, chicken alfredo, German roasted pork knuckles, and of course, Costco's iconic rotisserie chicken.

ANYTHING SPECIAL IN THE FOOD COURT?

Some items are familiar, like the hot-dog-and-soda combo (all pork, as in Australia and Asia) and cheese and pepperoni pizzas. There's also a unique pizza topped with barbecued chicken and feta cheese. You can get Korean style spicy fried chicken wings with Korean barbecue sauce and French fries — both of which are fantastic — and, in the beverage department, mango smoothies and taro milk tea, both offered with or without boba. If you are in the mood for dessert, you can order soft serve vanilla ice cream with chocolate or wildberry sauce topping.

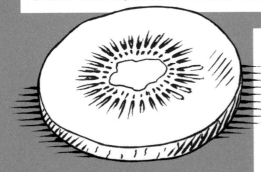

DOES COSTCO NEW ZEALAND HAVE ANCILLARY BUSINESSES?

Yes, the warehouse in Auckland offers Pharmacy, Optical, and Hearing Aid services. There is also a large gas station, with 27 pumps, offering gasoline well below the local average price. As elsewhere, the lower pricing at Costco's pumps helps drive down prices at other gas stations. Sadly, the Auckland warehouse does not have a liquor license.

OPENINGS

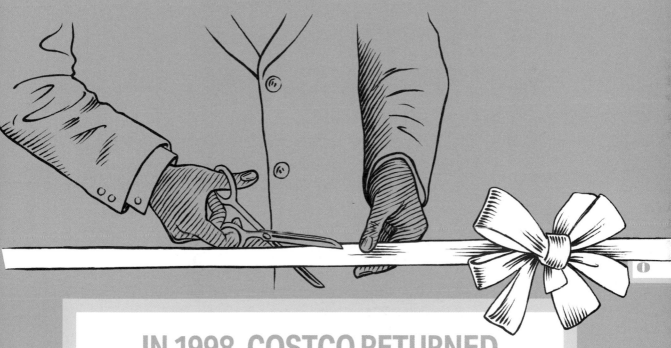

IN 1998, COSTCO RETURNED
TO THE MIDWEST AND
OPENED FIVE NEW
WAREHOUSES IN THE DETROIT
AREA ON THE SAME DAY

GRAND OPENINGS

On November 11, 2006 in La Quinta, California, Costco opened its 500th warehouse, bringing total sales floor area to 70 million square feet — approximately the same size as the combined flight deck space of 254 aircraft carriers.

Over the next 17 years, Costco opened another 350 warehouses, bringing the total to 850 by March 2023.

HOW LONG DOES IT TAKE FOR A NEW WAREHOUSE TO TURN A PROFIT?

Senior management is exceptionally patient, confident that over time the business will succeed. It took several years for the first Salt Lake City warehouse to reach target revenues, but inevitably local residents began to realize the value Costco brought to the area. Management's patience is usually rewarded by a strong revenue stream and loyal membership. In its early days, Costco's initial expansion in the Midwest was met with a lack of interest and the company withdrew, still considered one of the most difficult decisions management ever had to make. The return some years later was dramatic and successful. [SEE "INTRODUCTION"]

HOW DOES COSTCO DECIDE WHERE TO LOCATE A NEW WAREHOUSE?

Costco's Real Estate team is always on the lookout for new locations; when considering a new site, they analyze demographics, shopping, even cell phone usage patterns. The entire process can take months, or even years, based upon real estate pricing and availability, local governance, and other issues. If there is not yet a warehouse in your area, it is not because Costco hasn't considered it; rather, they have not yet found the right location.

HOW LARGE IS THE DEVELOPMENT TEAM FOR AN OVERSEAS EXPANSION?

The initial international team is surprisingly small, given the responsibility involved. Costco will appoint a country manager, head merchant, head of operations, and a finance director to handle the first phase of an international expansion. Two benefits of opening so many new warehouses overseas are the transfer and promotional opportunities for current employees.

HOW DOES COSTCO GENERATE MEMBERSHIP FOR A NEW WAREHOUSE?

Costco relies on social media, press coverage, and local signage to generate interest and drive member enrollments. In entirely new regions or countries, management may need to explain the benefits of the membership business model. Pre-opening day new member sign-ups are usually strong, but can really soar if a warehouse was long-anticipated or is in a completely new country. In Iceland in 2017, new sign-ups topped 100,000; China in 2019 doubled that at 200,000.

WHAT HAPPENS AT A WAREHOUSE GRAND OPENING?

The night before the opening, Costco hosts a party for employees, vendors, local VIPs, and press. Guests enjoy free hot dogs and soda at the Food Court and, in the Bakery, there's a large opening day cake with the store name and number on it. A long-standing tradition is the good-natured competition to guess opening day sales. The next morning, eager members line up early for the ribbon-cutting ceremony and to be the among the first inside the new warehouse. In Japan, there might be a *Kagami Biraki* ceremony, during which honored guests smash open large wooden kegs of sake for good luck. [SEE "JAPAN"] In China, opening day ceremonies have included traditional dancing dragon puppets and drum percussionists. [SEE "CHINA"] Opening days usually feature limited quantities of extra-special merchandise, like the latest version of a popular video game, high-end jewelry, or designer sunglasses. The CEO and other representatives from the Home Office attend every one of the 20-25 openings each year, regardless of the travel involved.

IN 2012, COSTCO SHIPPED 6 MILLION PAIRS OF GLASSES AND 7 MILLION BOXES OF CONTACT LENSES WORLDWIDE

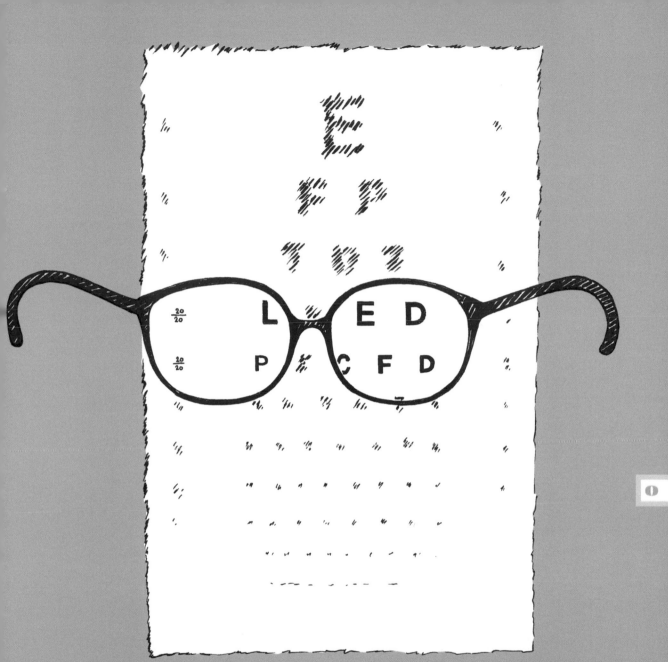

OPTICAL

WHAT OPTICAL SERVICES DOES COSTCO PROVIDE?

Eye exams are available at most Costco warehouses either by appointment or on a walk-in basis. Membership is not required to get an eye exam, but is necessary to purchase glasses or contact lenses. A Costco eye exam is not required for members to purchase optical merchandise, but a prescription written within the past year is mandatory. The optometrists at Costco are fully licensed and lease space at the warehouse; the other Optical department staff are employed by Costco.

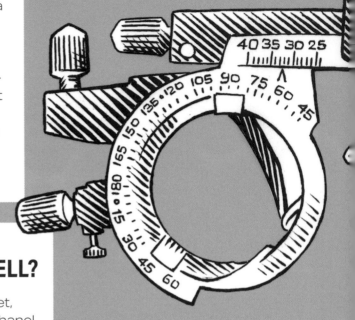

WHAT KIND OF GLASSES DOES COSTCO OPTICAL SELL?

Costco offers glasses for every budget, including upscale brands like Gucci, Chanel, Prada, and Burberry, and in many formats — progressives, high index, and polarized or traditional sunglasses. Costco purchases the frames from Luxottica, the largest eyeglass company in the world, and then manufactures the lenses, using the most modern composite materials. Members may bring frames bought elsewhere, for a small additional fee.

ARE THERE "WOW" ITEMS IN THE OPTICAL DEPARTMENT, TOO?

Keep your eyes peeled! In 2022, we spotted rhinestone-studded Gucci sunglasses in Stockholm for $500 and Saint Laurent shades in Sydney for $240. As with all things Costco, these items rotate; you never know what you might find.

HOW ARE OVERSEAS OPTICAL DEPARTMENTS SUPPLIED?

The Auburn, Washington optical lab supports Costco warehouses in Australia, Taiwan, Spain, and the UK. Even with shipping costs included, Costco delivers savings on glasses to overseas members versus local vendors. For example, supplying Australia with glasses saves 28% for members Down Under. In Japan, however, Costco cuts lenses in the individual warehouses, delivering prescription glasses in only thirty minutes. **[SEE "JAPAN"]**

WHERE DOES COSTCO PRODUCE LENSES?

There are four facilities in North America — two in the US (Auburn, Washington and National City, California), and one each in Canada and Mexico. Previously, there was a plant in Tukwila, Washington, which quadrupled in size and then moved to Auburn, in October 2016. The two US labs have more than 1,500 employees, working round the clock.

WORLD WAR II VETERAN JOHN HARRIS STARTED THE FIRST OPTICAL BUSINESS FOR SOL PRICE AT FEDMART

HOW DOES COSTCO PRICE THEIR EYEGLASSES SO AFFORDABLY AND YET MAINTAIN HIGH QUALITY?

Optical was the first vertically integrated operation at Costco. By 2018, increased automation of single vision lenses allowed Costco to cut costs 22%, which translated to $25 million in member savings. By reducing the manufacturing time for a pair of glasses, Costco has been able to increase production from 6,000 pairs of glasses per day to 9,000, yet still employs more than 600 people for quality control and safety monitoring. *Consumer Reports* consistently rates Costco — out of some 33 national optical shops — the best place to buy glasses, considering factors like the quality of frames and lenses, price, customer service, and the quality of fitting. This combination of high quality and low prices explains the popularity of Costco's Optical department. When combined with the Hearing Center, these two businesses generate $1 billion annually — among the highest sales per foot in the warehouse, except perhaps for Jewelry.

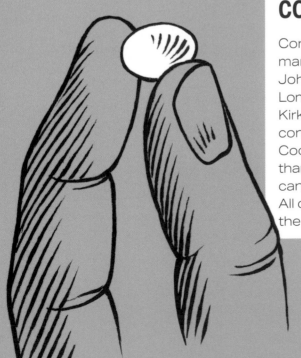

DOES COSTCO ALSO SELL CONTACT LENSES?

Contact lenses are sourced from major manufacturers like Alcon, CooperVision, Johnson & Johnson, and Bausch & Lomb. Members can also purchase Kirkland Signature daily disposable contact lenses (manufactured by CooperVision) in a 90-pack, for less than $60 — about $.66 per pair — which can be 15-35% less than other brands. All contact lens orders are processed in the same facilities as glasses.

PARKING LOTS

EVEN THE PARKING SPOTS
ARE SUPER-SIZED AT COSTCO —
ABOUT TWO FEET WIDER THAN
MOST OTHER RETAILERS

WHY IS IT SO HARD TO FIND A PARKING SPOT AT COSTCO?

The problem is not the size of the parking lots, because they usually have room for about 750 vehicles — it's an issue of popularity and demand! On the bright side, after you have found a spot, it is easier to maneuver in and out, with less chance of getting a ding in a car door because, at ten feet wide, Costco's parking spaces are about two feet wider than at most other retailers.

HOW DOES COSTCO DEAL WITH SITUATIONS WHERE THERE SIMPLY IS NOT ENOUGH ROOM FOR A PARKING LOT?

In some cases, the lack of parking space is a deal breaker and renders a location unsuitable for a warehouse. In densely populated urban areas (Asia, for example), the solution is vertical, with multi-story warehouses combining layers of parking and shopping within a single building. In some Korean warehouses, Costco contracts with nearby parking lots for extra spaces for members. In Vancouver, British Columbia, the warehouse was built underneath two luxury condo towers with the underground parking shared by residents and shoppers. In Santa Fe, Mexico, the warehouse complex includes a multi-story parking garage alongside the warehouse, topped with an athletic field and other community spaces. [SEE "MEXICO"]

WHO IS RESPONSIBLE FOR PARKING LOT DESIGN AND MAINTENANCE, ESPECIALLY THE LANDSCAPING?

Parking lots and their landscaping contribute to the overall shopping experience for members and matter to the surrounding community, as well. Costco usually spends at least 5% more on landscaping than is required by local authorities. Maintaining the landscaping is an important responsibility of the warehouse general manager. While "pulling weeds" refers to relocating items that have been left in the wrong area *inside* a warehouse, it also refers to pulling weeds *outside*, retrieving abandoned shopping carts and keeping the parking lot area in tip-top shape.

[SEE "LINGO"]

ARE THERE ACCOMMODATIONS FOR UNUSUAL VEHICLES?

In Lancaster, Pennsylvania, where a portion of the members who shop at Costco come from the Amish community, there is an area for horse-and-buggy parking, complete with brooms, shovels, and garbage cans for manure cleanup. We've seen many pickup trucks, which fit easily into the ten-foot-wide spots, and even a motorcycle with a small rear storage compartment, proving you don't have to shop in bulk at Costco!

P

PET SUPPLIES

COSTCO SELLS LOTS OF
PET SUPPLIES: FOOD, BEDDING,
TOYS, PRESCRIPTION DRUGS —
AND INSURANCE, TOO!

WHEN AND WHY DID COSTCO GET INTO PET SUPPLIES?

Costco has sold pet supplies almost from the day it opened. In 2020, the American Veterinary Medical Association estimated annual pet spending was $100 billion, almost 40% of which was for pet food, with about 63 million households owning a dog. Costco's pet supplies may be in the far reaches of the warehouse, but they usually occupy an entire aisle, filled with Costco sized-and-priced bags of food for dogs, cats, and birds.

DOES COSTCO SELL NON-FOOD PET SUPPLIES?

Costco sells veterinary prescription drugs at their pharmacies, and pet insurance through Chicago-based FIGO Pet Insurance. At some warehouses, Costco also sells branded dog toys, such as a party-pack of Costco-themed soft fabric toys in the shape of a bottle of vodka ("Dogka") or KS wine ("Whine"). Cat treehouses and scratch pillars are also available from time to time. Absorbent pads for house-training dogs, and kitty litter for cats, are almost always for sale, as are dog chews, collars, leashes, poop bags, and selected accessories. Costco also sells high-quality KS dog beds for about one-third the price at most other retailers.

DOES COSTCO SELL KIRKLAND SIGNATURE PET FOOD?

In 1996, two years after Kirkland Signature was launched, Costco began selling KS pet food, starting with a dry lamb-and-rice recipe for dogs and a maintenance meal for cats. Since then, the KS dog food line has expanded, with more than ten different formulas now available in 20- and 35-pound bags. Each flavor pairs a vegetable with a protein source — salmon, chicken, turkey, or beef — to balance out the meal, and is specially formulated for dogs of different sizes, ages, and dietary needs. Around the world, besides the KS line, Costco also sells major national brands of pet foods and supplies.

P

PHARMACY

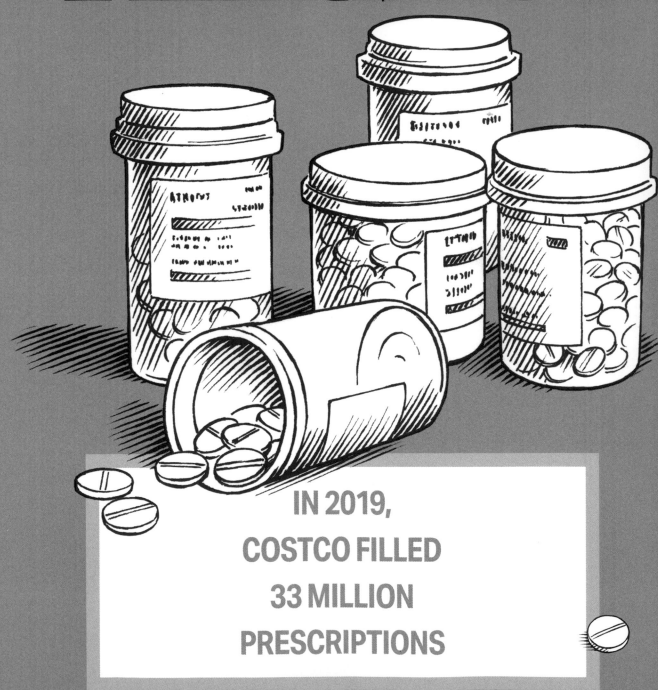

IN 2019,
COSTCO FILLED
33 MILLION
PRESCRIPTIONS

HOW MUCH CHEAPER ARE GENERIC DRUGS AT COSTCO?

In 2013, a Tampa, Florida local news station ran a story comparing Costco's pricing on generic drugs to the national chain drugstores. When the story was picked up by local stations across the country and CBS morning national news, it solidified Costco's pricing authority. National drugstore chains generally price generics at a discount on name brand drugs. Costco uses the same pricing model for drugs as for other products: with a minimal markup over cost. As of March 2023, based on 90-count quantities, the pricing for generic versions of five common drugs was staggeringly lower at our local Costco warehouse than at a national chain drugstore.

HOW DID COSTCO GET INVOLVED IN THE PHARMACY BUSINESS?

In 1986, Jim Sinegal and Jeff Brotman recruited Charlie Burnett to launch Costco's first Pharmacy, at the Portland, Oregon warehouse. Jim knew Charlie from their FedMart days where, over fourteen years, Charlie worked his way up from staff pharmacist to VP Pharmacy Operations. After FedMart closed in 1982, Charlie opened and ran four independent pharmacies in San Diego until Jim and Jeff convinced him to join Costco. They were intent on offering members high quality products at great prices and getting into the health and beauty aid business (HABA). Although Charlie retired from Costco in 2013, the pharmacy business continues to thrive. Sadly, Charlie passed away in June 2017.

P

HOW ARE PRESCRIPTIONS FILLED AT COSTCO?

Prescriptions are filled either at a Costco warehouse or at one of four central "fill centers," which are run jointly with the two wholesale drug companies that supply the drugs. The drug companies lease the buildings, operate the machinery, and stock the inventory under the supervision of Costco pharmacists. Using the fill centers to augment the warehouse pharmacies reduces patient wait times and operating costs, and also improves patient care in the warehouse, leaving more time for clinical screenings, immunizations, and consultations.

PETS ARE CONSIDERED FAMILY AT COSTCO: MANY PHARMACY LOCATIONS FILL PRESCRIPTIONS FOR DOGS AND CATS!

GENERIC DRUG PRICE COMPARISON:
National Drugstore Chain vs. Costco
90-DAY SUPPLY, WITHOUT INSURANCE

PRESCRIPTION DRUG	NATIONAL CHAIN	COSTCO	% SAVINGS
GENERIC ACTOS 30 MG	$588	$19	97%
GENERIC LEXAPRO 20 MG	$183	$15	92%
GENERIC LIPITOR 20 MG	$372	$26	93%
GENERIC PLAVIX 75 MG	$330	$11	97%
GENERIC SINGULAIR 10 MG	$312	$13	96%
	$1,785	$84	95%

DOES COSTCO ALSO SELL SPECIALTY DRUGS?

Two special fill centers — in Corona, California and Jeffersonville, Indiana — handle expensive specialty medications that may involve prior authorization and follow-up monitoring for side effects (e.g., cancer, MS, HIV, Hepatitis C, and other auto-immune diseases). The fill centers' staff go beyond the usual pharmacy services, helping with complicated pre-authorizations and keeping tabs on coupon availability to help ease the cost of these specialty medications.

ARE COSTCO PHARMACISTS FULLY TRAINED AND LICENSED?

Of course! Because of the licensing requirements, this is one department where Costco will make an exception to its general promote-from-within policy and hire managers from the outside. However, there are also opportunities for unlicensed employees to learn the business while working under the super-vision of a licensed pharmacist. Some employees take advantage of Costco's scholarship program to return to school and get a license. At least 25-30 Costco pharmacists started their careers pushing carts in the parking lot or working at the Food Court!

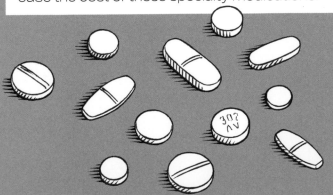

PRODUCE

COSTCO SOURCES ITS
PRODUCE FROM 44 DIFFERENT
COUNTRIES

WHEN DID COSTCO BEGIN SELLING PRODUCE?

In 1987, Costco founding officers Stan McMurray and Tim Rose began introducing fresh foods: meat, bakery, and produce. By 1991, to offer the freshest items at the lowest possible prices, Costco was sourcing as much produce as possible directly from growers. Frank Padilla, a young produce buyer who was the first to negotiate directly with individual farms, became the VP of Meat and Produce for Costco worldwide. In 2009, Costco sold $2.5 billion of produce, a significant portion of which was organic. Generally, the top-selling items are avocados and strawberries, followed by blueberries, raspberries, red grapes, and bananas. Since 2015, Costco has been the largest retailer of organic produce in the world, selling even more than Whole Foods.

HOW IS QUALITY ASSURED? WHAT HAPPENS TO SUB-PAR PRODUCT?

Costco's biggest produce challenge is to ensure that it arrives at the warehouse in top condition. Each item has unique specifications that are checked upon delivery at the depot, before the product is accepted from a vendor. For example, at a New Jersey depot we watched employees check the temperature of a shipment of strawberries with a handheld digital thermometer. (Sadly, the shipment was rejected.) If not within spec, the product is re-routed by the supplier to another retailer with different specifications. Once at the warehouse, produce is stacked on pallets to minimize bruising and is frequently checked for quality. If an item looks like it is no longer at its peak, it is culled, frozen, and sent either to a food bank or an animal sanctuary.

WHAT ARE SOME UNUSUAL PRODUCE ITEMS?

Costco was the first retailer to sell full-size seedless watermelons to US consumers. In recent years, Costco has sold a unique grapefruit called Melo Gold, a cross between a pomelo and a white grapefruit, less acidic than regular grapefruit and virtually seedless. Kiwi berries — grape-size kiwis with edible skin — are sold during a very short season in September. We delighted in pineberries, a hybrid white strawberry first developed in South America, which turns a slight pinkish hue when ripe. In Australia, Costco sells apple bananas, which are usually only available at local farmers markets. [SEE "AUSTRALIA"]

COSTCO SELLS OVER SIX MILLION PUMPKIN PIES BETWEEN SEPTEMBER AND DECEMBER EACH YEAR

PUMPKIN PIE

THEY TASTE GREAT! WHAT'S THE SECRET?

It wouldn't be a secret if we told you! Although we can tell you that the recipe relies on Dickinson pumpkins, a variety grown on more than 50,000 acres of Illinois farmland, which produces 565 million pounds of pumpkin per year — as much as the next five states combined.

P

HOW FAST DO COSTCO PUMPKIN PIES SELL?

An astounding two million are sold in the days leading up to Thanksgiving. Two locations in California's Central Valley — Visalia and Fresno — usually win the good-natured competition to sell the most pies per year, with a record 50,000 sold at each of these warehouses right before Thanksgiving. At the busiest locations, this can mean selling up to 900 pumpkin pies per hour! Fortunately, the pies freeze exceptionally well, so devoted fans can stock up during the season. Its return in the fall is joyfully heralded on Twitter, Instagram, and other social media.

FOR THE BIRDS

At Costco, nothing goes to waste: the pumpkin seeds are sold to a bird-food manufacturer.

ARE THE PUMPKIN PIES HANDMADE?

The pie crusts are pressed into the pie tins by hand at the warehouse, using dough made at the central bakery commissary. For years the pumpkin filling was ladled by hand, but in 2017 Costco switched to a custom-made pie-filling device that has dramatically increased the production rate. A full rack of 24 pies can now be filled in five minutes rather than twenty-five. That kind of efficiency improvement and bulk ingredient purchasing are two of the ways Costco can afford to keep the price so low.

WHAT IS NEEDED TO MAKE SO MANY PUMPKIN PIES?

Twelve million pounds of canned pumpkin (from 1.2 million cans), 24 million eggs, a blend of spices, and a few other ingredients. The recipe was originally developed in 1987 by Sue McConnaha, then Costco's VP of Bakery Operations. When Costco increased the size from ten to twelve inches in 1990, the price went up from $4.99 to $5.99, and has stayed there ever since in spite of rising costs. Weighing in at 58 ounces, that's a mighty tasty bargain.

QUALITY

COSTCO'S ROTISSERIE CHICKEN
IS TIME-STAMPED AND
SOLD FOR ONLY TWO HOURS AFTER
IT COMES OUT OF THE OVEN

Q

WHEN COSTCO TALKS ABOUT QUALITY, WHAT DOES IT MEAN?

Quality is defined as the degree of excellence that something possesses. Costco wants its members to expect that they cannot buy higher-quality items at other retailers, and the company works hard to be a "pricing authority," well-respected for competitive prices. Kirkland Signature products must be as good as — or better than — the leading national brands *and* at a lower price. Quality extends to service as well: Costco members should feel that the service they get in the warehouse, online, or by phone is second to none.

HOW DOES COSTCO ENSURE FOOD QUALITY?

Food quality begins with sourcing. Vendors are carefully vetted and regularly audited. Long ago, Costco noticed that a supplier of butter cookies, to save money, was skimping on butter. The vendor's contract was immediately — and permanently — terminated. Upon delivery at the depots, products like strawberries are rigorously checked for ripeness, sweetness, and color. Once in the warehouse, anything past prime condition is removed from the sales floor. Each department has procedures and specifications to ensure quality is maintained. In the Deli, for example, there are binders with laminated pages displaying the proper way to prepare each item; on the walls are large posters with reminders about safety and food handling. Regular warehouse visits by senior management, along with the slogan, "Don't change the recipe!" help maintain consistency around the world.

LEADING BY EXAMPLE

Every Costco employee helps keep things neat and tidy, including senior management, who lead by example, picking up any stray items on the floor during walk-throughs.

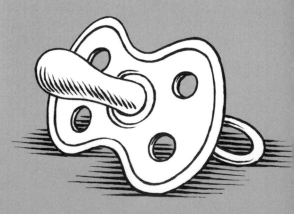

HOW DOES COSTCO'S DEDICATION TO QUALITY GREET MEMBERS?

At Costco, quality begins in the well-maintained, carefully landscaped parking lots, with their oversized parking spots. Except in South Korea — where local law strictly enforces opening hours — warehouse doors often open ahead of official opening time with the warehouse "show-time ready," as if the curtain were about to go up at a Broadway theater. Employees are expected to smile, make eye contact, and welcome Costco members to their club. Costco may be a "no frills" operation, but there is no skimping on the care of members. Senior management walks the warehouse floor at least once an hour to make sure pallets are neat, even, and straight, that the aisles are clean, that items are quickly replenished, and even to check temperatures of refrigerated goods. **[SEE "LINGO" AND "SOUTH KOREA"]**

WHAT DO KIRKLAND SIGNATURE DRESS SHIRTS AND COSTCO TRAVEL SERVICES HAVE IN COMMON?

Whether products or services, Costco goes to great lengths to ensure quality for its members. KS dress shirts are made of the finest Oxford cloth, with especially durable seams and buttons, and comfortable fit — all for a great price. The real "save story" of these shirts is that the original item sold for many times the price: over time, the product was improved even as management found ways to save on production costs to lower the price. Travel Department team members operate with the same approach. Every package deal offered by Costco Services has been experienced by a member of the team to assess quality and pricing. **[SEE THE SALMON STORY IN "FISH"]**

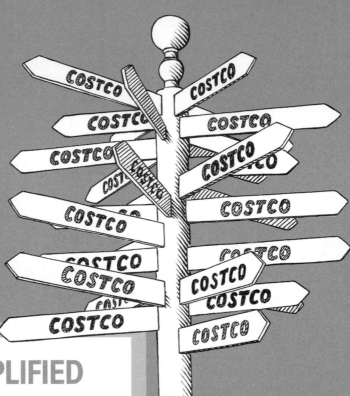

A SIMPLIFIED GUIDE FOR KEEPING TRACK OF COSTCO'S MORE THAN 850 WAREHOUSES AROUND THE WORLD

REGIONS

DOES EVERY STATE IN THE UNION HAVE A COSTCO WAREHOUSE?

As of March 30, 2023, Costco had more than 585 warehouses in 46 states — almost 70% of the 850 worldwide — organized into eight regions. The states without a warehouse: Maine, Rhode Island, West Virginia, and Wyoming. The corporate Home Office is in Issaquah, Washington in the Northwest regional office.

EIGHT COSTCO REGIONAL OFFICES IN THE US

	REGION	REGIONAL HOME OFFICE	INCLUDED IN THE REGION
BA	BAY AREA	LIVERMORE, CA	NORTHERN CALIFORNIA, NORTHERN NEVADA
LA	LOS ANGELES	GARDEN GROVE, CA	HAWAII, LOS ANGELES, SOUTHERN CALIFORNIA (EXCEPT SAN DIEGO)
MW	MIDWEST	OAK BROOK, IL	ILLINOIS, INDIANA, IOWA, KANSAS, KENTUCKY, MICHIGAN, MINNESOTA, MISSOURI, NEBRASKA, NORTH DAKOTA, OHIO, SOUTH DAKOTA, WISCONSIN
NE	NORTHEAST	STERLING, VA	CONNECTICUT, DELAWARE, MARYLAND, MASSACHUSETTS, NEW HAMPSHIRE, NEW JERSEY, NEW YORK, PENNSYLVANIA, VERMONT, VIRGINIA, WASHINGTON, DC
NW	NORTHWEST	ISSAQUAH, WA	ALASKA, IDAHO, MONTANA, OREGON, UTAH, WASHINGTON
SD	SAN DIEGO	SAN DIEGO, CA	ARIZONA, COLORADO, LAS VEGAS, NEW MEXICO, SAN DIEGO, SOUTHERN NEVADA
SE	SOUTHEAST	DULUTH, GA	ALABAMA, FLORIDA, GEORGIA, MISSISSIPPI, NORTH CAROLINA, PUERTO RICO, SOUTH CAROLINA, TENNESSEE
TE	TEXAS	PLANO, TX	ARKANSAS, LOUISIANA, OKLAHOMA, TEXAS

HOW MANY DIVISIONS DO THE ELEVEN REGIONS ROLL UP INTO?

The eleven Costco regions around the world are rolled up into five divisions: Eastern US, Southern US and Mexico, Western US, Northern US, and International, which includes Canada. (Please don't ask why Mexico is not part of International — it dates back to the Price Club days.) While every job at Costco is important, the executive vice presidents in charge of divisions are truly road warriors, traveling a LOT to keep up with the warehouses in their areas.

WHICH STATES HAVE THE MOST COSTCO WAREHOUSES?

Ten lucky states contain almost 60% of the total 585 warehouses in the US. In case you are planning a road trip and want to target a Costco-rich state, you might want to give extra consideration to one of these states, which were the top ten as of March 30, 2023 [SEE "YONKERS TO YORBA LINDA"]

STATE	# OF WAREHOUSES	% OF US WAREHOUSES
CALIFORNIA	133	23%
TEXAS	37	6%
WASHINGTON	33	6%
FLORIDA	30	5%
ILLINOIS	23	4%
NEW JERSEY	21	4%
NEW YORK	19	3%
ARIZONA	19	3%
VIRGINIA	17	3%
GEORGIA	16	3%

Please be forewarned that Costco opens 20-25 new warehouses each year, so things may well change.

STATE WITH the MOST COSTCOS

HOW ARE REGIONS ORGANIZED OUTSIDE THE US?

As of March 30, 2023, there were Costco warehouses in 13 countries outside the United States: Australia, Canada, China, France, Iceland, Japan, Mexico, New Zealand, South Korea, Spain, Sweden, Taiwan, and the United Kingdom (England, Scotland, and Wales), but by the time you are reading this, there may well be more! Outside the US, Costco warehouses are organized into three regions: Asia, Australia/New Zealand, and Europe, which includes the UK, France, Spain, Iceland and Sweden.

SOUTH KOREA

Illustration of sculpture
by Kyungmin Kim,
Gwangmyeong, South Korea

S

AN EXOTIC MULTI-LEVEL
TREASURE HUNT

WHY AND HOW DID COSTCO OPEN IN SOUTH KOREA?

South Korea is a prosperous country the size of Virginia, with a population of over 50 million. Dating back to the early 1950s when the US defended South Korea against invasion, Koreans love all things American. (There are still 15 US military bases in the country, so the servicemen and their families are also potential Costco members.) Just as the Price Club/Costco merger was taking place in 1993, Price Club was concluding an agreement with the Korean retailing conglomerate Shinsegae; Shinsegae would own the operation, while Price Club would license its name and run the operation. On October 7, 1994, the first Korean warehouse opened, in Seoul's Yangpyung neighborhood, under the well-known Price Club banner — even though by that time the Prices had left the merged company. At 94,000 square feet, Yangpyung is the second-smallest warehouse in the Costco system, with parking above the main retail floor. As of May, 2023, there were 18 Costco warehouses in South Korea.

WHAT ARE SOME OF THE CHALLENGES OVERCOME BY COSTCO IN KOREA?

During the 1997 Asian banking crisis, South Korea's currency dropped more than 53% almost overnight, making imports prohibitively expensive. In its wake, Shinsegae sold a majority stake to Costco, gradually reducing its ownership to 3.3%, which Costco purchased in 2017. Costco was able to regain momentum after the 1997 financial crisis and the currency gradually recovered. Costco still faces some competition from E-Mart, which is owned by Shinsegae, and Lotte, both of which are far less curated, and stock close to 100,000 SKUs (versus Costco's 3,800 items). In other countries, Costco typically likes to open a bit early as a courtesy to members, but that practice is prohibited in Korea because businesses must strictly adhere to advertised business hours. Costco also closes every other Sunday in deference to local small businesses. In compliance with Korea's Art Decoration Law, which requires 0.7% of construction funds for any large building be spent on public art, Costco has installed fantastic sculptures in front of many warehouses.

HOW DOES THE FRESH FOOD COMPARE TO THE US?

Korean bulgogi (literally "fire beef") is prepared daily in the Deli section and is also on offer at the Food Court as a pizza topping. Beef tongue, sold whole and sliced, is also quite popular, especially for barbecuing. The Deli has many *banchan* (side dishes) and two unique "kits": spicey Korean shabu-shabu and stir-fried tripe. The seafood section is overwhelming, much of it locally sourced. There are live lobsters and crabs, littleneck clams, abalone, blanched fresh octopus, squid, and fish. In the Deli section there's a wide range of sushi, seasoned pollock and crab, fresh rockfish, and stews, including octopus/seafood. The Bakery sells *a lot* of bagels and other typical American Costco baked goods, but also more unusual items like a fresh melon mousse cake, Earl Grey tea muffins, red bean buns, and a deliciously rich fig bread.

COSTCO IN SOUTH KOREA SELLS
KIMCHI
REFRIGERATORS
THAT REPLICATE ANCIENT
UNDERGROUND
CURING CONDITIONS.

MOST KOREAN FAMILIES
OWN AT LEAST ONE!

LOOKING FOR LIQUOR AND SNACKS FOR A PARTY?

The alcohol section, like others in Asia, is stocked with fine wines and spirits from around the world, as well as Japanese sake and Korean distilled *soju*, which is not to be confused with Japanese *shochu: soju* is made from a variety of different grains or potatoes; unlike *shochu*, it is sold in a wide potency range, from 25 to 100 proof. Korean snacks like rice crackers and seaweed crisps, black sesame crispy rolls, and tofu crackers dominate the snack section. Koreans also love dried seaweed and dried seafood items like squid strips and abalone chunks.

핫도그세트 ₩2,000
HOT DOG SET
HOT DOG + SODA

ANY SPECIAL PRODUCTS AT THE SOUTH KOREAN WAREHOUSES?

South Korea has become well-known for its skincare products and regimens; Costco sells a lot of these high-end "K-Beauty" products. We saw a few wonderful ladies' clothing Road Shows while in South Korea. [SEE "LINGO"] There are plenty of high-end watches, from Chopard, Breitling, Hublot, and the like, ranging in price from $17,000-30,000, or a 5.23 carat diamond ring with a platinum band for about $236,000. The Food Courts have a few noteworthy tasty items — mushroom soup, calzone, and fresh watermelon juice — and offer a choice of reusable tableware for dining in or disposable items for take-away.

ARE THE WAREHOUSES SIMILAR TO THOSE IN THE US?

Korea is very mountainous, rendering about 70% of the land uninhabitable, and urban areas are densely populated. Many of the warehouses in Korea are multi-story, with large moving ramps that connect floors, like an airport's moving sidewalk but much wider, and on an incline. The cart's wheels lock to hold it safely in place while on the ramp. In the unfortunate event that a ramp breaks down, the staff covers the ramp with red carpeting and members can still use it — with the cart's wheels unlocked, of course — but with some extra effort. As members use these multi-level conveyors, they are entertained by illuminated advertising panels on the warehouse walls.

WHAT IS CHUSEOK?

Chuseok is an important holiday celebrating the mid-autumn full moon — usually in September — shared with friends and family, honoring ancestors. Koreans exchange "gift sets" — elaborate presents that might feature Spam or dried seaweed, live lobsters or wagyu beef — which are available at all retailers. We happened to visit South Korea the weekend before Chuseok and the range of gift sets at Costco was truly impressive.

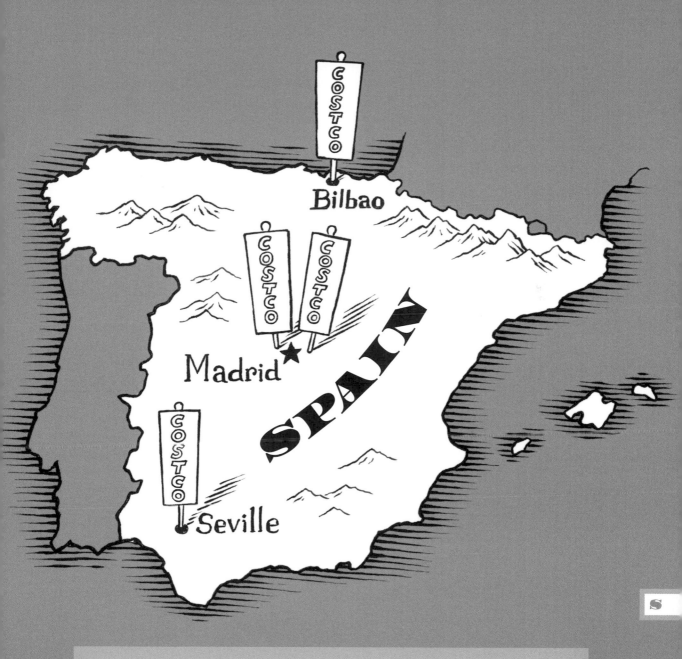

IN 2014, THE FIRST EUROPEAN
COSTCO OPENED IN SEVILLE

WHY DID IT TAKE SO LONG FOR COSTCO TO OPEN ON THE EUROPEAN CONTINENT?

In the 1990s and 2000s, Spain enjoyed rapid economic growth, becoming the fifth largest EU economy, but Costco was focused on Pan-Asian expansion, where there were fewer regulatory restrictions and less opposition from local retailers. After the 2008 global credit crisis, Costco turned its focus to Europe. Spain presented an attractive opportunity with a population of 47 million and a $1.4 trillion GDP. In 2013, Spain's unemployment was at a record 34% when Costco began hiring: almost 150,000 people applied for the 250 jobs, which then paid roughly twice as much as minimum wage. On May 15, 2014, twenty-one years after opening in the UK, Costco finally opened its first European warehouse, in Seville, Spain's fourth largest city. By 2022, three more warehouses had opened: two in Madrid, the Spanish capital, and one in Bilbao, the most populous Basque city, in northern Spain.

HOW ARE SPANISH COSTCO WAREHOUSES SUPPLIED?

Purchasing is handled in three places: locally for Spanish merchandise; Watford, England for European items; and the Seattle Home Office for global purchases. Specialty items like Kirkland Signature Spanish saffron and Ortiz tuna are also exported to the rest of the Costco global network. Costco may build a depot in Spain, after the number of warehouses has increased.

SPAIN IS FAMOUS FOR ITS SEAFOOD — HOW IS THE SELECTION AT COSTCO?

Spanish cuisine is seafood-heavy, and Costco has a wide variety of locally sourced seafood, including crab, cuttlefish, razor clams, sea bass, whole octopus and squid, salmon, and Galician turbot — a flat fish called *gallego* in Spanish. Perhaps most interesting is the range of prawns and other shellfish which are key ingredients in paella, commonly known as Spain's national dish, originally from Valencia.

SMALL BUSINESSES REPRESENT ABOUT 40% OF COSTCO'S BUSINESS IN SPAIN

WHAT ARE TAPAS AND DOES COSTCO SELL THEM?

Tapas are small servings of snacks or appetizers like olives, nuts, or cured ham, usually served with drinks. Costco in Spain sells rare "Bellota" cured pork from black-footed Iberian pigs — fed only sweet acorns — prized by gourmets for the pork's sweet subtle flavor. Costco's price is less than half what you might pay elsewhere. It's sold pre-sliced, but there are also Costco-sized portions — entire pork legs — hanging from special racks in the Deli. There is a large selection of smoked fish, caviar, salsa, guacamole, olives, and other cured meats for tapas time, too.

DOES COSTCO SELL WINE AND SPIRITS IN SPAIN?

There's a wide range of wines and spirits for tapas, with professional sommeliers on hand. Two unusual gin varieties are orange-flavored Tanqueray Sevilla, and Tanqueray Malacca, flavored with an exotic mix of botanicals and spices, produced in very limited quantities. One of the most expensive items we saw was a six-liter bottle (known as a Methuselah) of Louis Roederer Cristal 2002 Champagne, selling for a very reasonable $9,000 — several thousand dollars less than the price elsewhere.

HOW DOES THE FRESH FOOD IN SPAIN COMPARE WITH OTHER COSTCO WAREHOUSES?

It's a good mixture of American standards and unique Spanish fare, about two-thirds locally sourced. For example, right next to the classic rotisserie chicken, there are roast pork knuckles and pork ribs, time-stamped and sold heated, for a limited amount of time to ensure quality. In fresh meat, there is domestic beef, pork, and lamb alongside Canadian Angus. In the Deli section, we *loved* the freshly made *pastel salado*, a popular Spanish luncheon item. Costco's version alternates layers of seafood salad, bread, and cream cheese, topped with smoked salmon. Amidst produce from Mexico, Brazil, Peru, and the US was locally sourced *chirimoya*, a small tropical fruit that tastes like pineapple, which is usually grown in South America. Another unusual Produce item: bottled coconut smoothies.

WHAT'S ON THE MENU AT THE SPANISH FOOD COURT?

The Food Court has a larger, more diverse menu than Costco in the US, including Cobb salad, chicken fingers, a basket of BBQ chicken wings, cheeseburgers, and French fries. Our favorite item was *croquetas de jamon:* small, breaded, deep-fried tapas filled with melted cheese and pieces of cured ham — totally worth the calories! For dessert, enjoy ice cream sundaes with chocolate, caramel, or fruit.

ARE THERE ANY DIFFERENCES IN THE BAKERY VERSUS COSTCO IN THE US?

In addition to familiar American items, Spanish Costco bakeries sell distinctive Spanish sweet treats like *milhoja de crema* (millefeuille with cream), strawberry cheesecake, *tarta de dulce de leche,* chocolate biscuit cake, and unusual savory items like tuna empañada or ham-and-cheese-filled puff pastries. Seasonal items include *Pan de Muerto,* a sweet soft bread covered with sugar crystals served for the Day of the Dead (November 1st and 2nd), and a dense Christmas fruit cake.

ANY NOTEWORTHY NON-FOOD ITEMS?

Spaniards are very active, and there is lots of sporting equipment for sale, such as rowing machines, bikes, basketball arcades, and an air hockey table. You could also buy a mini electric Vespa for your kids, a Pac-Man arcade, or a Fender guitar or ukelele. There are no Business Centers in Spain, so regular warehouses stock items like large commercial refrigerator units or an LED lit *Abierto* ("Open") sign. In 2021, there was a display case with high-end handbags from designers like Moschino and Valentino.

SUSTAINABILITY

AS A RESULT OF INSTALLING
A WATER METERING SYSTEM,
COSTCO HAS REDUCED ITS WATER
CONSUMPTION BY 22%

WHAT ARE SOME EXAMPLES OF HOW COSTCO RECYCLES?

Costco recycling is evident throughout the organization and involves many different materials. In e-commerce, Costco is striving to reach 100% recycled materials for delivery cartons. Kirkland Signature spice bottles consist of 50% recycled material. In produce, apples are packed in recycled corrugated boxes and mushrooms in recycled molded fiber baskets. In the Food Court, plates are made of recycled material; Costco no longer uses plastic straws for drinks; and the hot dogs are now wrapped in a paper bag instead of paper/foil wrap. For over a decade, Costco has sought to reduce use of polystyrene (Styrofoam®) in packing materials used by the fresh food department. To date, some 80 fewer truckloads of polystyrene are going to landfills each year, and recycling of the remaining polystyrene has increased by over 15%.

FRANZ LAZARUS

After college and a stint as a Vista volunteer, Franz joined FedMart. He opened and managed FedMart's store on an Arizona Navajo reservation, then worked at Price Club. In November 1983, Jim Sinegal and Jeff Brotman hired Franz as Costco's Director of Operations. He set up the East Coast division and, in 1994, when Costco increased international expansion, Franz spent the next 15 years overseas as the EVP/COO International Operations. At one point he briefly retired, but returned to Costco to run HR, Administration, and Sustainability. Aside from finance, there is no area of the business in which he didn't work.

Franz officially retired in August 2019.

WHEN DID COSTCO BEGIN ADDRESSING SUSTAINABILITY?

In October 1987, the United Nations published the Brundtland Report (also known as "Our Common Future"), defining sustainable development as that which "meets the needs of the present without compromising the ability of future generations to meet their own needs." Yet four years before that report was even issued, Costco was already recycling its cardboard. In the spring of 2007, well aware of the potential impact of their global business, Costco established a Corporate Sustainability Department. It was led by Franz Lazarus, Senior VP, Administration for Global Operations and Corporate Sustainability, and mandated to make decisions that made sense from a business perspective without negatively impacting the environment or society.

HOW IS COSTCO REDUCING ITS CARBON FOOTPRINT?

In 2007, solar arrays installed at two Costco warehouses provided 15-20% of the annual power, eliminating more than two million pounds of carbon emissions each year. The 2015 change from round to square containers for Costco's nuts improved packing efficiency — more containers per pallet — thereby reducing the number of truckloads by some 400 annually, and another 200 fewer truckloads a year from Costco's shift to plastic pouches. Other savings are generated by using the heat from refrigeration systems to preheat hot water tanks, and replacing concrete with prefabricated industrial metal buildings to provide better insulation. Between 2016 and 2020, Costco estimates it reduced its carbon footprint by 32% when adjusted for the growth of its business, including all gasoline vehicles and refrigeration equipment. We could go on, but you get the picture.

HOW DO LITTLE CHANGES IN PACKAGING DELIVER BIG RESULTS?

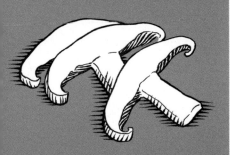

Costco estimates that changes in packaging over the past few years have resulted in a total reduction of about 17 million pounds of plastic annually, and the process continues. Minor modifications at a company the size of Costco can have enormous impact. For example, changing the packaging for Kirkland Signature laundry detergent from a rigid plastic tub to a flexible plastic bag resulted in a reduction of 1.6 million pounds of plastic annually. Moving from plastic clamshells to corrugated cardboard boxes for apples reduced the use of plastic by some 11 million pounds annually. Costco's 16.9 ounce water bottle — already made with recycled plastic — was modified to have a slimmer plastic cap; because Costco sells so many of those water bottles, that slight modification saves hundreds of thousands of pounds of plastic annually.

ANY INTERESTING SUSTAINABILITY INITIATIVES IN THE PIPELINE?

Costco is working to reduce emissions from refrigeration units by experimenting with alternate coolants designed to release fewer hydrocarbons into the atmosphere. Costco's coffee roasting facility in New Jersey spent extra money to install a second cleaner for the exhaust pipe to prevent pollutants from being vented into the atmosphere during the roasting process. Costco's multi-year Climate Action Plan has accelerated the phase-out of HFCs, calls for upgraded refrigeration units to reduce refrigerant emission by 30% by 2030, and increases Costco's program to purchase renewable electricity.

CAN YOU SHARE A FEW SUSTAINABILITY SUCCESS STORIES?

The grease from the rotisserie chicken process is turned into bio-fuel. Food scraps from the Deli, Meat and Bakery departments are sold to farmers for use as animal feed or crop fertilizer. In 2020, Costco recycled 6.5 million tires and over 600,000 tons of cardboard and plastic wrap. In the US and Canada, Costco warehouse receipt paper is now phenol-free.

HOW DO COSTCO'S VENDORS CONTRIBUTE TO SUSTAINABILITY?

Costco works directly with suppliers to improve sustainability of manufacturing and packaging (and insists that vendors pay their own employees a fair wage and treat them as well as Costco treats its own employees). Suppliers involved in Kirkland Signature coffee products must maintain a Fair Trade certification for their products, ensuring that coffee workers are not being exploited. For other commodities like vanilla and honey, Costco partners with local supply chain managers to ensure that the crops are sustainably developed — and that workers have access to clean water and healthy food, and are paid fairly for their labor.

SWEDEN

LAGOM ACCURATELY DESCRIBES COSTCO'S CURATED PRODUCT SELECTION

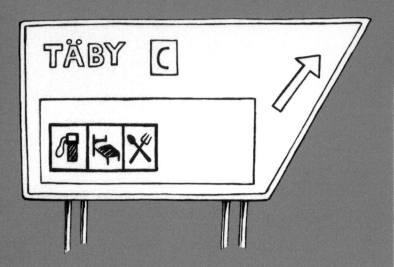

HOW IS PRODUCT SENT TO SWEDEN?

Merchandise is either shipped from the UK or Rotterdam, or sourced locally. Domestic items arrive by truck. Merchandise that is purchased at the Home Office in Seattle is shipped from the East Coast of the US to Watford and then to Sweden. About two-thirds of Swedish Costco merchandise is locally sourced.

IS IT LAGOM?

Lagom is a Swedish word that means "just the right amount." It could be applied to the number of SKUs at a Costco warehouse or, more generally, to the typical Swede's philosophy of life: not too much, not too little. [SEE "LINGO"]

HEJ! HEJ! COSTCO IN SWEDEN?

In 2019, nearly half a million Swedes visited the US; many experienced Costco firsthand and loved it. On October 27, 2022, Costco opened its first Swedish warehouse in a busy shopping mall in Täby, a prosperous suburb just north of Stockholm. Since the cost of living is high in Sweden, Costco's business model of high-quality items at the lowest possible prices is very attractive to Swedish shoppers. Costco Sweden is able to offer optical, audiology, and pharmacy services, and has a tire service center, but the sale of alcohol is highly regulated. Outside of *Systembolaget* — government-owned liquor stores — alcohol may only be sold to licensed resellers such as restaurants, bars, and hotels.

IS THE PACKAGED FOOD DIFFERENT FROM THE US?

Sweden is supplied from UK Regional Office in Watford, so a lot of the packaged food is British, like Cadbury chocolate or HP Sauce. There are also popular Swedish items like flat rye crackers, often served with a topping of caviar paste, gravadlax, pickled herring, or smoked salmon. Of note at the opening was a 700-gram Belgian chocolate caramel "popcorn bar" selling for about $15, which was too large for our carry-on luggage, so we shipped it home!

HOW IS THE SWEDISH PRODUCE SELECTION?

The harsh Swedish winters have engendered a love of root vegetables, especially radishes, onions, and potatoes; the latter is served with most main courses, and all the root vegetables are sourced locally. As in Iceland, radishes are sold in two-pound bags and are sweeter than in the US.

WHAT IS THE SWEDISH MEAT DEPARTMENT LIKE?

The meat selection is extensive — much of it domestic — and includes beef and pork. Cured pork and sausages are popular in Sweden; Costco has a good range of these items from domestic sources. Irish beef is also sold, including a huge "tomahawk" beef chop. Cured ham is popular in Sweden, so Costco offers a variety of cured ham products, including rare Iberico Bellota. [SEE "SPAIN"]

DOES COSTCO IN SWEDEN SELL ANYTHING FOR *FIKA*?

A sacred part of Swedish life, *fika* refers to taking a break for a drink and snack with friends or co-workers. *Fika* includes any beverage of your choice, but it's usually coffee: after Finland, Sweden has the second highest coffee per capita consumption in the world. Costco in Sweden sells a full range of coffees and a staggering array of baked goods for *fika*. [SEE "BAKERY"] Preparing for Sweden's National Cinnamon Bun Day on October 4th, your choice for *fika* provisions should be obvious!

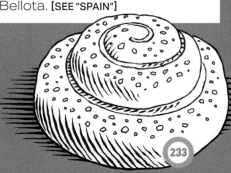

S

HOW DOES COSTCO'S SWEDISH FISH AND SEAFOOD DIFFER FROM OTHER PLACES?

Seafood is a large part of the Swedish diet and Costco has a fantastic array including monkfish tails, Swedish crabs, lobsters, scallops, and oysters. In October 2022, one of the most popular items at the grand opening was unshelled, cooked King Prawn crevettes. In the days before food was readily imported year-round, Swedes came to rely on pickling and curing fish (and meat). Costco Sweden sells several varieties of smoked salmon and gravadlax — which is cured rather than smoked — including Kirkland Signature smoked salmon. Pickled herring is another staple, and Costco sells several different varieties. Caviar is popular and reasonably priced versus US prices. Costco also sells domestic fish roe in a tube, which can be used as a spread on bread or crackers.

FUTURE GROWTH FOR COSTCO IN SWEDEN?

With a population of 10 million, Sweden can probably sustain seven or eight warehouses. As of 2023, a second warehouse was planned for Malmö, a major city in southern Sweden, to open within a few years. More will likely follow.

ANY UNUSUAL ITEMS?

Snus (tobacco snuff) is illegal throughout the EU except in Sweden. Costco offers a wide variety of locally produced brands in colorful cans, displayed in a special refrigerator unit. Swedish snuff is not snorted. It's a fine powder combining ground tobacco, water, and salt: a pinch is placed between the lip and gum. For the Costco opening we attended, the smallest but most expensive item in the warehouse was a 6.55 carat round brilliant solitaire diamond ring labeled "one of a kind," selling for almost $500,000.

OPENING CEREMONIES FOR
TAIWANESE COSTCO WAREHOUSES
CAN INVOLVE LION DANCING,
BARREL-SIZED DRUMS, AND
LARGE ORANGE DRAGONS

T

WHAT'S THE DIFFERENCE BETWEEN THE REPUBLIC OF CHINA (ROC) AND THE PEOPLE'S REPUBLIC OF CHINA (PRC)?

Taiwan (the ROC) was established in 1949 after Chiang Kai-shek's Nationalist forces lost the civil war on mainland China (the PRC) to Communist leader Mao Tse-tung. The Nationalists fled to Taiwan, an island southeast of the PRC. Think of the two countries as David and Goliath: Taiwan (13,974 square miles, 24 million residents) versus China (1.4 *billion* residents, almost 4 million square miles spanning five time zones). Though Taiwan consists of 168 islands, 99% of Taiwanese live on the main island, once known as Formosa. Since 1949, Taiwan has developed into a vibrant democracy with a prosperous economy.

WHEN DID COSTCO BEGIN DOING BUSINESS IN TAIWAN?

In 1994, Costco manager Richard Chang — a recently hired Taiwan national who had played basketball at UC Berkeley and then professionally in Taiwan — moved from San Diego back to his home country. In 1995, Costco teamed up with President, owner of Taiwan's first department store chain, to launch in Taiwan. In January 1997, Costco opened its first warehouse in the port city of Kaohsiung, Taiwan's second largest city. In 2022, Costco bought out President's 45% stake in the joint venture for just over $1 billion. As of May 2023, Taiwan has 14 Costco warehouses and a depot, all located along the island's densely populated west coast; Richard Chang is the SVP for Costco in Asia.

ARE THERE SPECIAL ITEMS IN FRESH FOOD?

USDA Prime and Choice beef are popular in Taiwan, but there is also a wide selection of pork, lamb, and chicken, including cut-up, fresh, black-skinned Silkie chicken, which has been part of Chinese cuisine for thousands of years. Another unusual find is USDA Choice heel muscle beef, very popular when braised because it includes beef tendon. As in other Asian countries, the assortment of seafood and sushi is overwhelming. Two of our favorite fish items were kabayaki salmon belly and seasoned conger eel, both fully cooked and totally delicious. In the Deli section, the rotisserie chicken — with its head still on — is packaged in clear plastic bags, instead of the rigid plastic containers used elsewhere, and sold alongside roasted pork knuckles and irresistible Hakka salted pork. The Deli section has tasty prepared "kits" such as Japanese pork ramen and Singapore Laksa (a spicy noodle dish topped with various meats), and a host of fresh salads. Produce ranges from familiar Western items like celery and asparagus to more exotic Asian fare like water bamboo, white water snowflake (the stems of a flowering water plant), and organic jelly ear mushrooms, which are brown and gelatinous.

TAIWAN COSTCO WAREHOUSES SELL LOCALLY MANUFACTURED KAOLIANG, A VERSION OF BAIJIU (SORGHUM SPIRITS), WHICH PACKS QUITE A PUNCH AT 58% ALCOHOL

ANY SPECIAL SUSTAINABILITY INITIATIVES IN TAIWAN?

The Sinjhuang warehouse, opened on January 7, 2017, has 100% LED lighting and parking garage lights powered by solar roof panels — an initiative later adopted in many other Taiwanese warehouses.

ANY OTHER SPECIAL FOOD ITEMS?

Much of the packaged food is sourced locally and is truly unique. For example, golden kimchi, flavored with carrots, is sweeter and milder than standard kimchi. The Bakery featured many desserts with fresh fruit: fruit trifle, cantaloupe cake, and strawberry peach cheesecake in addition to standard Costco items like muffins and croissants. Dinner rolls injected with butter, ready to heat up and serve, and chocolate chip bagels were both a surprise.

WHAT ARE SOME OF THE CHALLENGES OF OPERATING IN TAIWAN?

The main challenge was getting locals to embrace Costco's business model: a membership warehouse with high quality goods at tremendous savings. Taiwan's warehouses are now among the busiest in the system. The preference for rotisserie chickens with heads still attached required special rotisserie equipment. The highly mountainous terrain means that urban space is densely populated and priced at a premium. Warehouses are multi-story, with multiple floors for shopping and several parking levels, either above or below the main shopping areas. Members travel between floors on inclined moving ramps which lock the wheels of members' carts to prevent slipping on the ramp. A potentially temporary challenge is that until China generates enough business to warrant its own depot and regional office, the burden for supporting China remains on the Taiwan Costco systems. [SEE "CHINA"]

ARE THERE DIFFERENCES IN THE FOOD COURT?

As in other Asian countries, the hot dogs are pure pork. In addition to standard cheese pizza, Taiwan also sells "Hawaiian" (pineapple), combo, and seafood variants. Other items are delicious clam chowder, a chicken Caesar salad, chicken or bulgogi bakes, irresistible crispy spicy chicken, and a pesto chicken sandwich. Beverages include iced or hot coffee, latte or Americano. Don't miss out on the superb chocolate soft serve ice cream.

ANY NOTEWORTHY COSTCO LOCATIONS IN TAIWAN?

By transferring current employees to help open new warehouses, Costco is able to maintain its unique culture so the warehouse will probably feel familiar even though you are far from the US. After you've been to Costco warehouses in Taipei, other locations are also worth a visit. For example, the Hsinchu warehouse (#5001), about an hour outside the capital city of Taipei, is located in an area considered to be the "Silicon Valley" of Taiwan. Opened on August 23, 2022, the Tainan warehouse (#5008), is located in one of Taiwan's oldest cities, which has an abundance of Buddhist and Taoist temples.

TIRE CENTERS

COSTCO IS ONE OF
THE LARGEST RETAILERS
OF TIRES IN THE US

WHEN DID COSTCO START SELLING TIRES?

In 1978, Price Club began selling high quality tires at lower prices than the competition as another way to bring members into the warehouse. For many years, the business was managed by Sol Price's older son, Larry. It was successful in the US and was later expanded to Canada and Mexico. After the Price Club/Costco merger, the Tire Centers were continued and, space permitting, are in most warehouses today.

WHAT MAKES THE TIRE CENTERS SO POPULAR?

Costco sells Bridgestone, Michelin, and Goodrich tires at prices that are very competitive. The tires are filled with nitrogen, which retains its pressure longer than compressed air, thereby extending the life of the tires. Costco also offers a five-year road hazard warranty against damage while driving — over and above the manufacturer's warranty — which comes with free regular services such as rotation, balance, and nitrogen refill. Without this warranty, the cost of rotation, balancing, and nitrogen refill is about $20. Appointments can be scheduled online or in person.

ANY TIRE MAINTENANCE TIPS?

If you replace one front tire, don't be surprised if your tires are rotated and the new tire is placed in the rear. Safety experts advise that if tires are unevenly worn, it is preferable to place the newest tire in back.

COSTCO SELLS A LOT OF TIRES. HOW DOES THIS BENEFIT THE MEMBERS?

Here's one of our favorite examples: a tire manufacturer gave Costco a $1 million dollar rebate because of the large volume of tires that had been sold. Without getting approval from the Seattle Home Office, the rebate was distributed to every member who had purchased tires — even though it involved a lot of research and paper-work for the Tire Center employees.

UNITED KINGDOM

IN 1993, COSTCO'S FIRST WAREHOUSE OUTSIDE OF NORTH AMERICA OPENED IN A LONDON SUBURB

U

ANY SIGNIFICANT DIFFERENCES IN THE UK COSTCO BUSINESS MODEL VERSUS THE US?

Anyone can purchase a Costco membership in the US; however, the UK government requires at least 60-65% of business must be with trade members (e.g., owners of "corner shops," which are known as convenience stores in the US). Almost 70% of the Liverpool warehouse's business is in trade. On weekdays, trade members can enter the warehouse earlier than individual members.

WHY DID COSTCO SELECT THE UK FOR ITS FIRST OVERSEAS FORAY? HOW WAS THE RECEPTION?

The UK, historically dominated by three large retailers — Sainsbury, Tesco, and Safeway — had little pricing competition. Prior to the merger with Costco, Price Club had formed a partnership with Littlewoods, one of the UK's largest private retailers, to explore entry into the UK. Post-merger, Costco proceeded with the UK launch in partnership with Littlewoods and Carrefour, each of whom had 20% equity. (Both partners were later bought out.) Sainsbury, Tesco, and Safeway contested in court that Costco wasn't truly a wholesale operation, but rather a standard retail business and as such, subject to more stringent regulations. The competitors failed to have Costco's planning approval revoked, generating considerable advance publicity about Costco's arrival. On November 30, 1993, Costco opened its first British warehouse in West Thurrock, about 12 miles east of Central London. Astoundingly, the Sainsbury/Tesco/Safeway trio reignited the Costco buzz by publicly bemoaning the attention they'd drawn to their competitor during the court battle. As of May 2023, there are 29 Costco warehouses in the UK, a depot, and a regional office which also oversees and supports operations in France, Spain, and Iceland.

DO THE UK WAREHOUSES LOOK THE SAME AS AMERICAN ONES?

Most UK warehouses look similar to those in the US, except the Stevenage warehouse, about 15 miles north of Central London, which opened July 24, 2019. This Costco is in a repurposed John Lewis department store distribution center built in 1963, which was listed on the British registry of historic sites for its historical/architectural importance in 1995. The building's interior is stunning, with its original, delicate, elegant columns, and a low-slung ceiling in parts of the building too low to accommodate Costco's traditional shelving. A minor, but notable difference versus the US: product shelving is yellow and black instead of the typical orange and green.

THE READING, ENGLAND WAREHOUSE IS CLOSE TO WINDSOR CASTLE AND BUCKINGHAM PALACE AND SUPPOSEDLY PROVIDES PRODUCTS TO BOTH LOCATIONS

ANY WAREHOUSES WITH LOCAL SPECIALTIES?

The Aberdeen warehouse in Scotland sells fresh haggis, a type of sausage stuffed with sheep's innards, oatmeal, and spices, or a "buttery" — a traditional Scottish bread roll that provides sustenance to sailors. The Bristol, England, warehouse sells four different brands of cider, all made within close distance of the warehouse; the Birmingham, England, warehouse sells Banks's Original Beer, which is brewed a mere 12 miles away. If you want to buy Henderson's Relish Pack — known as "Hendo's" — you will need to visit the South Yorkshire warehouse in Sheffield, England, the only Costco that carries this condiment, which is produced nearby and is similar in appearance to Worcestershire sauce, but without anchovies.

HOW DO THE BAKERY ITEMS COMPARE TO THE US?

In addition to the standard Costco Bakery items, UK warehouses also sell some very British desserts, like: mini-mince pies stuffed with sultanas; fresh cream mini-Victoria sandwiches; a posh luxury fruit cake; some French-influenced items like profiteroles or a sumptuous Black Forest *gâteau;* and a very large, very American carrot cake. In Scotland, members can buy Walker's Highland Oat Cakes or potato scones to accompany their tea.

ARE THE FOOD PRODUCTS IN THE UK THE SAME AS IN THE US?

About 60% of the products are domestically sourced, including some obvious favorites like Marmite, a uniquely British salty yeast spread, which in 2022 was sold in a two-pound plastic tub for about $6. There was also a four-pack of 240 PG Tips tea bags for only $14 (about a penny per bag). UK warehouses carry products from local vendors such as: Trewithen Dairy's traditional Cornish clotted cream; Heritage Breeds' Duchess Pearl free-range duck eggs; or a two-pack of three-quarter-pound glass jars of Hazlemere free-range goose fat. The fresh Meat and Fish departments proudly display Aberdeen Angus beef and bright-yellow-dyed smoked haddock fillets. UK Deli sections have Kirkland Signature versions of British favorites like beef stew with dumplings or chicken hot pot, as well as international options like chicken tikka masala or a hoisin duck and pancake kit.

WHAT IS ON OFFER AT THE FOOD COURT?

The UK Food Court menu is more extensive than in the US. Perhaps the two most unusual items are an Aberdeen Angus cottage pie — minced beef and onions topped with mashed potatoes and cheesy herb crumbs — and "jacket potatoes" — baked potatoes with a choice of toppings, like tuna salad, shredded cheese, baked beans, or beef chili. A few other different items: Korean beef BBQ bake, fish-and-chips, chicken tenders, double chicken fillet sandwich, cheese-burger, and French fries.

HOW ABOUT ANCILLARY BUSINESSES LIKE OPTICAL, AUDIOLOGY, AND PHARMACY?

You will find an Optical department and a Hearing Aid Center, both offering the same great products at very good prices. However, because of regulatory restrictions, warehouses in Britain do not have pharmacies. They do, however, offer the same types of over-the-counter health and beauty aid products that you find in the US, including Kirkland Signature vitamins and supplements.

ANY UNIQUE GIN-RELATED ITEMS AT COSTCO?

The British traditional affection for gin, purportedly the UK's most popular alcohol beverage, means that there are more varieties of gin at Costco warehouses in the UK than in a typical American warehouse. At the holidays, there is even a gin Advent calendar with a different small bottle of gin for each day, and a gift box with gin-filled glass Christmas tree ornaments. One of our favorite 2022 holiday items at Costco was a light-up Glitter Globe filled with orange and gingerbread gin liqueur, made in the UK that sold for about $20.

VENDORS

COSTCO HAS A UNIQUELY
COLLABORATIVE PHILOSOPHY:
"WHEN OUR SUPPLIERS
DO WELL, WE DO WELL"

WHAT DOES IT TAKE TO BECOME A COSTCO VENDOR?

All Costco suppliers, regardless of size, must be able to provide sufficient volume of consistently high-quality goods at a price that represents an extraordinary value — and they must adhere to Costco's Vendor Code of Ethics. Whether a smaller artisanal supplier selling at select local warehouses or a multinational company with global distribution, the only restriction is that Costco may not represent more than 25% of a vendor's business. New vendors routinely approach Costco, but are also discovered at trade shows or through social media or, in some instances, by warehouse managers simply asking current employees what products they enjoy at home that are not being sold at Costco.

CAN YOU GIVE ME SOME EXAMPLES OF LOCAL BUYING?

Buyers in Hawaii work with some 50 local vendors to source over 200 SKUs. **[SEE "HAWAII"]** This might be only 5% of the total number of SKUs, but is one of the reasons we find it so interesting to visit Costco warehouses around the world. If successful, and a vendor can handle the increased volume, local products may, over time, be sold at Costco warehouses nationally or internationally. A special case: in 2020, when the pandemic brought Hawaii's tourist trade to an abrupt halt, Costco partnered with Honolulu Cookie Company (HCC) to sell the company's highly perishable delicious inventory of butter cookies at Costco warehouses within the sell-by date. Hawaiian retail shops are back in business, but HCC's product line is also now available at select Costco warehouses around the world.

WHAT IS COSTCO'S VENDOR CODE OF CONDUCT?

A detailed five-page document, the Vendor Code of Ethics aligns with Costco's own internal guidelines. **[SEE "CODE OF ETHICS"]** There are three areas of focus: labor practices, workplace conditions, and product improvement. Underage and slave labor are strictly forbidden, and work environments must *at least* be in complete compliance with all laws. An unusual part of the code is that vendors must be committed to continuous product improvement to reach "above and beyond" goals of manufacturing, quality, and efficiency. **[SEE "QUALITY"]**

LABELS

Costco's non-foods department develops product labeling standards that meet or exceed state and federal regulations, preferring to use terms like "water resistant" instead of "waterproof" to reduce consumer confusion.

HOW DOES COSTCO MONITOR VENDOR COMPLIANCE WITH THE CODE OF ETHICS?

Costco sells only 3,800 SKUs; they need to be safe, reliable, and traceable. Costco's buyers perform regular business audits, and quality assurance teams at 12 labs around the world routinely evaluate product safety; goods for children 14 years of age or younger have additional testing. Independent auditors conduct "social audits" to monitor employee treatment, sustainability, safety, and environmental concerns; compliance is mandatory for all vendors. If issues are identified, Costco works with the supplier to develop a corrective action plan.

WHAT IS "PRACTICAL USE" TESTING?

Products that require assembly or are high on the D&D list (damaged and donated) may be selected for practical use testing. Buyers replicate the customers' experience: they purchase an item, use the enclosed instructions and tools for assembly, check if everything is included in the box and that no special tools are required for actual assembly. After that, product performance is evaluated, especially with usage over time.

WHAT'S THE SECRET TO SOURCING "WOW" ITEMS?

It's a two-way street: buyers may suggest a red wine Advent Calendar to a vendor, or it may be the vendor's idea to create gin-filled Christmas tree ornaments. Only Costco and its vendors know for sure whose idea something was. Holidays like Halloween can be a "wow" extravaganza at Costco: in recent years, we've enjoyed seeing full-size animatronic witches stirring a brew pot, or scarecrow banjo players for sale in warehouses around the world. For Chuseok, South Korea's major mid-autumn harvest festival, vendors begin working with Costco well in advance to design and produce "gift sets" uniquely for Costco, ranging from a Spam sampler to live lobsters or wagyu beef. [SEE "SOUTH KOREA"]

HOW DOES COSTCO LEVEL THE PLAYING FIELD FOR SMALLER VENDORS?

Once a year, at the International Managers Meeting in Seattle, select vendors are invited to show their products — sort of like a preview of in-warehouse sampling, but for warehouse managers from around the world. This kind of global exposure helps smaller vendors compete with giant companies like Proctor & Gamble. New or smaller vendors may also be invited to do a local Roadshow [SEE "LINGO"] as a product test that creates excitement for members. In 2006, Wet Noses Dog Food was successful at such a Roadshow; by 2014, their product was in Costco warehouse distribution and their workforce had increased from two to fifty-five employees.

CAN YOU EXPLAIN "VENDOR PARTNERSHIP"?

Ideally, Costco's relationship with vendors is a productive partnership with ideas flowing back and forth. New products are always being sent to Costco for consideration, but Costco might also suggest a new product idea to a current vendor. Sydney-based vendors CAL Marketing, for example, have worked this way with Costco for over a decade, manufacturing a wide range of Asia-themed snacks — like dried shiitake mushrooms or coconut rolls — for global distribution. Costco's buyers visit production facilities or farms all over the world, working together to improve efficiency and quality while reducing production costs, which benefits vendors and Costco members alike.

WALL STREET

COSTCO IS MANAGED
FOR THE BENEFIT OF MEMBERS,
EMPLOYEES, VENDORS,
AND SHAREHOLDERS

HOW DOES WALL STREET VIEW COSTCO?

For a time, some financial analysts and commentators looked down on Costco for cutting prices whenever possible and leaving potential profit on the table, but Wall Street finally understands and appreciates Costco's unique business model. The company's basic principles originated with Sol Price, back in the FedMart days: obey the law, do right by members, take care of employees, and respect vendors. Those core principles have enabled Costco to enhance shareholder value to an extent that few other companies have, while saving money for members and providing high wages for employees.

HOW DOES CUTTING PRICES ENHANCE SHAREHOLDER VALUE?

Cutting prices as much as possible and giving money back to members is deeply ingrained in the firm's culture and one of the main reasons members are so loyal. Membership renewal rates are about 90% annually and yearly membership growth generally remains at a steady 6%. The Tire Rebate story is but one example of Costco's approach. Years ago, Costco in Canada sold so many tires that the manufacturer gave Costco a $1 million rebate. Instead of pocketing the windfall, Costco painstakingly tracked down every member who had bought the product and sent each one a check with a portion of the rebate. A short-sighted analyst might argue that this decision reduced shareholder profits, but it actually cemented the company's relationship with the members who unexpectedly received rebate checks, enhancing their loyalty to Costco and increasing sales in the long run.

SINCE GOING PUBLIC IN 1985, **COSTCO STOCK HAS DRAMATICALLY AND CONSISTENTLY OUTPACED BOTH THE DOW JONES INDUSTRIAL AVERAGE AND THE S&P 500**

251

RICHARD A. GALANTI

The son and nephew of grocery store operators, Richard Galanti was part of the team of young bankers from New York-based investment bank DLJ that led Costco's second round of fundraising. Jim Sinegal and Jeff Brotman were so impressed with Richard that they hired him as VP of Finance in March 1984, and promoted him to senior VP, Chief Financial Officer within one year. In January 1995, Richard became a director.

He is one of the longest-serving CFOs of a Fortune 500 company.

HOW DOES TAKING CARE OF EMPLOYEES ENHANCE SHAREHOLDER VALUE?

Costco pays its employees better than most other comparable retailers, but not in an altruistic way. Rather, a highly paid workforce is not only happy, but stays on the job. After the first year of employment, Costco's employee turnover is about 7% annually — one of the lowest in the retail industry — resulting in significant financial benefits for the firm and shareholders. For example, a large proportion of employees involved in logistics have been at Costco for many years, which enables them to find new ways to enhance efficiency and safety. In other words, treating employees well adds directly to the bottom line.

HOW DOES WALL STREET VIEW COSTCO'S "NO-FRILLS" BUSINESS CULTURE?

Costco's business culture is at the opposite end of the spectrum from most other Fortune 100 companies. The "board room" is an unadorned conference room at the Home Office, which has an open bullpen seating arrangement for even the most senior executives. Instead of a beautiful mahogany conference table, the board meets at four large folding tables (sold at Costco warehouses). Quarterly earnings calls are straightforward and informal, with CFO Richard Galanti ready and willing to give comprehensive answers to questions.

COSTCO'S LARGEST WAREHOUSE IS THE SIZE OF FOUR NFL FOOTBALL FIELDS!

WAREHOUSES

HOW WAS THE FIRST WAREHOUSE BUILT?

Quickly! The first Costco retail location — a pre-existing warehouse leased south of downtown Seattle — was retrofitted in only six weeks. The project was led by one of Costco's founding officers, Tom Walker, who ultimately served as Costco's EVP, Construction & Distribution for 21 years. He later succinctly explained Costco's preference, in the early days, for leasing rather than buying warehouses: "We were poor." [SEE "LOGISTICS"]

ARE ALL COSTCO WAREHOUSES THE SAME?

Definitely not! Unlike some other retailers, Costco designs each warehouse for its specific location, and works with the community to make modifications. For example, in Iceland, the roof of the warehouse is grass-covered, as a nod to historic thatched roofs and to soften the view from a nearby housing development. In France, the first Costco warehouse has an extraordinary "living wall." The Costco in Stevenage, England is a retrofitted warehouse with historical significance; care was taken to preserve the building. [SEE "AUSTRALIA," "FRANCE," "ICELAND," "MEXICO," AND "UK"]

WHERE ARE THE BIGGEST AND SMALLEST COSTCO WAREHOUSES?

At 235,000 square feet, the Salt Lake City Costco, which combines a regular warehouse and a Business Center, is the behemoth of all Costco warehouses, followed by the Tukwila, Washington Costco, which is the second largest and has an unusual interior layout, too. Head north to Juneau, Alaska to visit the smallest warehouse, which is a mere 74,052 square feet. The Juneau warehouse is the only one remaining from a 1993 test of smaller-size warehouses, so small it doesn't have rotisserie chicken ovens or its own Bakery. [SEE "ALASKA"] The Yangpyung warehouse in Seoul is the second smallest in the world at 94,000 square feet with multi-level retail floors. We're proud to share that our "home warehouse" in Manhattan is the third smallest at less than 100,000 square feet.

254

WHO DESIGNS AND BUILDS THE WAREHOUSES?

MG2, a Seattle-based architecture firm, has designed all of Costco warehouses. The main warehouse structure — most often steel construction — typically takes 45 days to erect, by six-man crews from Span Construction who put up the walls and roof with component parts fabricated by Butler Manufacturing. Both dedicated to continuous improvement, Span and Butler have constructed more than 116 million square feet of Costco facilities worldwide. After the walls are up and the roof is in place, local teams install shelving, electricals, plumbing, HVAC, refrigeration, and freezer units while work is completed on the fuel station, parking lot, and landscaping. The construction of a new warehouse from start to finish usually takes just 110 days, although during the pandemic it sometimes took longer.

ONCE A WAREHOUSE SITE IS IDENTIFIED WHAT ARE THE NEXT STEPS?

After Costco's Real Estate department identifies a site, it seeks approval from the CEO. If approved, the site gets "green inked." [SEE "LINGO"] Costco then works with relevant local stake-holders to obtain planning and construction approvals; the work begins as soon as possible. Costco uses regional general contractors, each one experienced in building to Costco's exacting specifications. The first step is to grade the site and prepare it for pouring the concrete base. Once concrete is poured and allowed to set, work begins on the warehouse itself.

WHAT ARE SOME CONSTRUCTION CHALLENGES COSTCO HAS FACED?

Although it might take relatively little time to build a warehouse, planning one may take years. All sorts of local factors come into play, including traffic control, wetland or wildlife preservation concerns, even an archaeological excavation, as occurred in San Francisco! In Hiroshima and New Orleans, before setting the foundation, pilings were driven down into bedrock to stabilize the warehouses. In Mettawa, Illinois, an underground storm-water retention system was built to drain 12 million gallons from a pre-existing lake. In 2006 in downtown Vancouver, Costco built a warehouse beneath a luxury residential apartment building, using steel pillars for structural support.

HOW HAVE WAREHOUSES CHANGED OVER TIME?

Costco prefers purpose-built warehouses on purchased land, but will occasionally retrofit an existing warehouse or move into a shopping mall (e.g., Reykjavik or Manhattan). Warehouse design has changed over time in a few significant ways:

INTERIORS ARE MUCH BRIGHTER AND LIGHTER
thanks to white paint on the interior walls and ceilings, skylights in up to 6% of the ceiling area, and brighter lighting fixtures.

CENTRAL AC WAS NOT STANDARD IN 1983
when Costco first opened, but since the mid-1990s, Costco's Energy Department works to keep all North American Costco locations at a comfortable 74°F year-round.

FRESH FOODS HAVE GROWN INTO A VERY SIGNIFICANT PORTION OF COSTCO'S BUSINESS,
with over two dozen "coffin-style" coolers in the Deli.

SHOPPING CARTS HAVE BEEN MOVED OUTSIDE
the warehouse and are stored under a canopy.

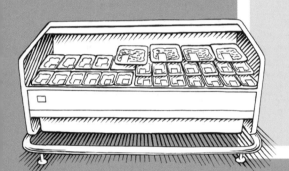

CHANGES IN WAREHOUSE DESIGN OVER TIME

	1983	2007
AVERAGE SQUARE FOOTAGE	108, 000	155, 000
TOTAL ACRES FOR THE LOT	6 – 8	12 – 18
# OF PARKING SPACES	400	750
STEEL CONFIGURATION	2 10'—HIGH TIERS	3 15'—HIGH TIERS
WIDTH OF MAIN AISLES	10'	12'

WINE & SPIRITS

IN 2019, COSTCO SOLD
A STAGGERING $4.8 BILLION
OF WINE AND SPIRITS

HOW DID COSTCO BECOME SUCH A MAJOR PLAYER IN WINE AND SPIRITS?

Back in the FedMart days, Sol Price was quite successful with private label liquor. In 1983, Annette Alvarez-Peters started working at Price Club in San Diego as an administrative assistant and receptionist. Over the next seven years, she worked as an inventory control specialist and assistant buyer before being promoted to Buyer for electronics. In 1995, two years after the Price Club/Costco merger, she moved to Los Angeles and became Buyer for Alcohol Beverages for 40 locations in Hawaii and Los Angeles, even though she was raised in a house with no drinking and knew little about fine wine. That year, Costco began buying classified-growth Bordeaux futures and is now the largest importer of this celebrated category. Over the years, Annette and her team built Costco's reputation and impact in the Alcohol Beverage market. By the time she retired in 2020, Annette was directing and assisting eleven regional and corporate buyers in the US and assisting nine international buyers. Working closely with selected vendors and offering only the best products at the best prices, Costco has become a significant player in the industry.

WHO MAKES KS WINES AND SPIRITS?

Kirkland Signature wines are sourced from vineyards around the world, including some legendary vineyards that have produced more wine than they can bottle themselves. Spirits are produced by major name brands and often sold for lower prices. The rumor that KS French vodka is produced by Grey Goose is untrue, although for a period of time Costco and Grey Goose both used water from the same source.

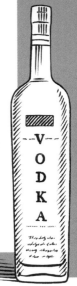

DOES EVERY COSTCO WAREHOUSE SELL FINE WINE AND SPIRITS?

The sale of alcohol beverages in the US is regulated state-by-state, by country overseas, and in some locations totally prohibited. In many states, alcohol is sold inside a Costco warehouse, which will include Kirkland Signature items, and in others it is sold in an adjacent outlet that often will not sell KS liquor. In Washington State, Costco joined the successful effort to have state regulations revised to permit the sale of spirits — in addition to wine — inside their warehouses. In Iceland and Sweden, Costco can only sell alcohol beverages to licensed commercial resellers.

WHAT'S COSTCO'S MOST POPULAR ITEM IN WINE AND SPIRITS?

This varies, but in many US warehouses KS American Vodka is the best-selling item. In Hawaii and Australia, beer is the top seller. In France and Spain, wine outsells hard spirits; the UK sells an impressive range of gin; in Japan, domestic whisky is the top-selling item.

TWO COSTCO WAREHOUSES ARE USUALLY IN THE TOP RANKINGS FOR LIQUOR SALES: PALM DESERT, CA AND SCOTTSDALE, AZ

DOES COSTCO EVER HAVE CELEBRITY LIQUOR EVENTS?

In 2019, chef Guy Fieri and rock star Sammy Hagar signed bottles of their special Santo Tequila Blanco at a California warehouse. The same year, actors Bryan Cranston and Aaron Paul handed out samples of Dos Hombres mezcal.

CAN YOU GIVE ME EXAMPLES OF "WOW" LIQUOR ITEMS?

Costco members know to buy something on the spot if it appeals, because the inventory always changes. In our travels, we've seen some amazing items, which may never be seen again, but here are some highlights. In the Scottsdale, Arizona warehouse, we were impressed by the whiskey selection, ranging from a $5,999 bottle of Balvenie single malt to a $26,999 bottle of Royal Salute 52-year-old blended scotch. In France we saw a Balthazar (12 liters) of Veuve Clicquot champagne for about $1,600. Surely, the sale of an entire barrel's worth of Jack Daniel's whiskey (22 cases with 12 bottles each) is in the running for the largest single sale of alcohol at a Costco warehouse. The member who bought it was having a special party indeed.

XALAPA

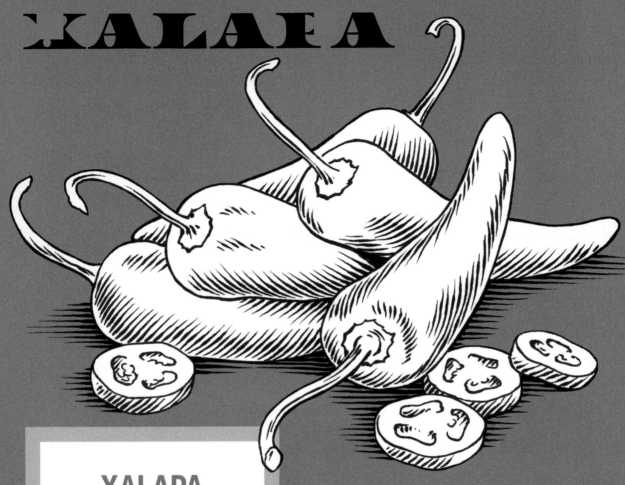

XALAPA PUTS THE "X" INTO "THE JOY OF COSTCO"

WHAT ARE THE MAJOR INDUSTRIES IN XALAPA?

It's nicknamed "The Flower Garden of Mexico" because flowers play such a vital role in the economy. Coffee and tobacco are grown and processed in Xalapa, and, of course, jalapeño peppers. As the state capital, the city is home to government workers and the University of Veracruz.

WHAT'S SPECIAL ABOUT THE XALAPA COSTCO?

Other than the happy fact that it begins with an "X"? The Xalapa warehouse opened on May 5, 2000; it's set into a hillside, with a large earthen wall behind it, palm trees in the parking lot, and an outdoor Food Court with a self-serve pickled-jalapeño-pepper dispenser. Inside the warehouse, you will find a wide range of outstanding Mexican food. Of particular note are two desserts: fresh strawberries with whipped cream and graham cracker crumbs, and Chocoflan, caramel flan atop a chocolate sponge cake base. Something truly unique in the Deli section is a six-pound package of fresh puff pastry for about $10 US. The Food Court attracts talkative Mexican zanate birds, also known as great-tailed grackles, who are grateful for any leftovers. [SEE "MEXICO"]

ARE THERE ANY OTHER TOURIST ATTRACTIONS BESIDES COSTCO?

Xalapa has an anthropological museum and a lovely botanical garden, Jardín Botánico Francisco Javier Clavijero. On a clear day, Pico de Orizaba, the highest volcano summit in North America, is visible from Xalapa; it is dormant, but not extinct. The port city of Veracruz — Mexico's version of Annapolis — is also worth visiting and has its own Costco, which opened in November 2005.

261

RESIDENTS ARE KNOWN AS EITHER XALAPEÑOS OR JALAPEÑOS.

THE FAMOUS PEPPER ORIGINALLY FROM THIS TOWN IS ONLY SPELLED ONE WAY.

CAN YOU DESCRIBE THE CITY OF XALAPA?

Xalapa, the capital of the Mexican state of Veracruz, is about a 90-minute drive inland from the port city of Veracruz, past lush sugar cane fields and grazing cattle. Xalapa's hilly narrow streets are bustling, with small shops that sell household goods, fresh flowers, meat, poultry, vegetables, and many different kinds of dried chili peppers. A beautiful 18th century cathedral overlooks the central square, and the dormant volcano Macuiltépec — now a lovely nature park — rises yet another 1,500 feet higher. The volcano has been inactive for so long, the crater has become a tropical jungle. According to legend, Xalapa was the birthplace of the world's most beautiful woman.

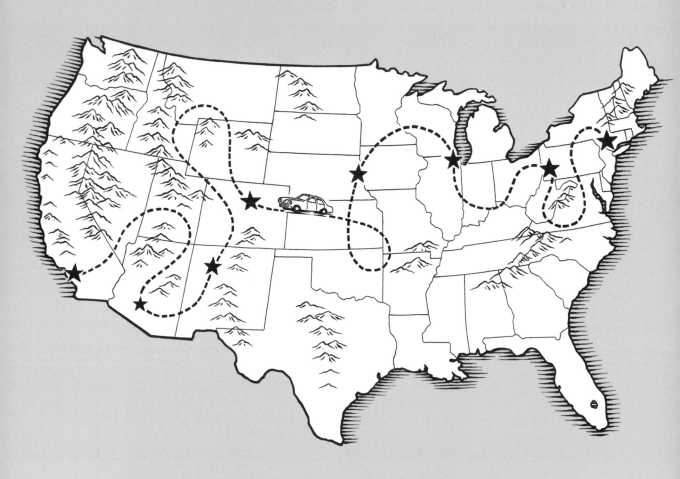

YONKERS TO YORBA LINDA

A COSTCO ROAD TRIP
FROM NEW YORK TO CALIFORNIA

WOULD YOU LIKE TO DRIVE ACROSS THE US, VISITING COSTCOS COAST TO COAST?

This itinerary will be great fun — and provide a "Y" section for our book! According to AAA, your 3,106 mile journey will require about 48 hours of driving, based on doing 5 – 7½ hours each day (350 – 475 miles). As of May 2023, the only states without at least one Costco warehouse were Maine, Rhode Island, West Virginia, and Wyoming. **SAFE TRAVELS!**

SHALL WE START AT YONKERS?

The Yonkers warehouse in suburban New York City, which opened on October 29, 1999, does not have a fuel station, but the nearby New Rochelle Costco does. Before you leave the NYC area, you might want to visit the third smallest Costco warehouse in the world. Located in Manhattan, it opened on November 12, 2009. You will have to pay to park, but it is one of the best parking deals in NYC.

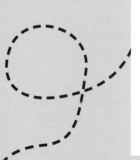

THE FIRST LEG: YONKERS TO PITTSBURGH

From Yonkers, you'll head to Pittsburgh via I-80 West, passing through the Delaware Water Gap. Prepare to be dazzled by the Christopher Columbus Scenic Highway, where the Delaware River cuts through the Appalachian Mountains. The entire 405-mile drive from Yonkers to the Robinson warehouse on Costco Drive, 12 miles west of Pittsburgh, should take about 6½ hours. This warehouse opened on July 9, 2002; it has a gas station, so you can fill up for the next segment of the journey.

PITTSBURGH TO THE WINDY CITY

Back on I-80 West, the next leg is 457 miles (about 7 hours) to Chicago, where you can choose from 21 Costco warehouses in the metropolitan area. On November 17, 1998, Costco first opened in suburban Chicago in Schaumburg and Oak Brook, but we would recommend the South Loop warehouse downtown (which has a gas station). If you have some extra time, you can also visit Willis Tower (formerly Sears Tower). On a clear day, from the 1,353-foot high Skydeck, you can see up to 50 miles and four states: Wisconsin, Illinois, Indiana, and Michigan — all of which have Costco warehouses.

CHICAGO TO OMAHA

Hope you filled up, because it's a 7½ hour drive (477 miles) from Chicago due west on I-80 to Omaha, Nebraska. There are two warehouses in Omaha, with a third one in the works. The La Vista warehouse, which opened on October 26, 2016, is closest to the highway. If you have any extra time in Omaha, you might want to visit the 160-acre Henry Doorly Zoo and Aquarium, which claims to have the world's largest indoor desert.

READY FOR A LONG DRIVE? OMAHA TO DENVER!

At 546 miles, this 8 hour drive is the longest leg of the journey. You will cross vast swaths of prairie land and climb the Rocky Mountains into the Mile High City. After so much driving, we'd recommend the Sheridan warehouse — opened on August 8, 2008 — because it is close to the highway and has a Tire Center, fuel station, and Food Court.

DENVER TO ALBUQUERQUE

This 6½ hour drive (446 miles) follows the Santa Fe Trail across the New Mexico border. The landscape is varied, with rugged mountains, expansive grasslands, and historic Old West towns. We would recommend visiting the oldest Costco warehouse in Albuquerque, originally a Price Club, which opened on December 1, 1984.

ALBUQUERQUE TO SCOTTSDALE

It's a 6½ hour drive (407 miles) from Albuquerque to Phoenix — which has ten Costco warehouses — and 11 miles further to the Scottsdale warehouse, which is not only near the highway, but is also reputed to sell the largest amount of fine wine and liquor in the world (although the Costco in Palm Desert is also popular for spirits). Scottsdale even has a professional sommelier — a Costco employee — in the liquor section, ready to help with your wine selection. Although Scottsdale has only one Costco warehouse, the city has over 200 golf courses!

GRANDE FINALE: SCOTTSDALE TO YORBA LINDA!

Happily, the final leg, at 5½ hours (369 miles), is the shortest. On the way to Yorba Linda, California, a beautiful town nestled in north-eastern Orange County — southeast of Los Angeles — you will drive through some of the most famous desert landscapes in the country, including Joshua Tree National Park. More important, you will also pass through Palm Springs where Jim Sinegal and Jeff Brotman first developed the business plan for Costco. And now, 23 miles southwest of Riverside — birthplace of the California citrus industry — you will reach your final destination, the Yorba Linda Costco. Proceed immediately to the Food Court for a celebratory hot dog!

WE
SOLVED
OUR
"Z"
PROBLEM!

ZAMA

WHAT IS ZAMA?

Zama is a suburb 25 miles southwest of Tokyo, Japan, where Costco opened a warehouse on December 10, 2011. Although the city has a relatively small population (about 130,000, as of June, 2021), there are two US military installations within three miles: the US Army base in Zama, and the US Naval Air facility in nearby Atsugi. Not surprisingly, the Zama warehouse has more foot traffic from American GIs and their families than any other Costco in Japan, and many employees are comfortable speaking English. Zama is only a one-hour train ride from central Tokyo.

HOW ARE THE MEAT, FISH, AND DELI DEPARTMENTS?

If you like wagyu beef, you will be overwhelmed by the choices and the great prices. The array of fresh and frozen fish and sea food is mind-boggling, with too many varieties to list. The Deli has some interesting new pre-cooked items, which simply need to be reheated at home, like Singapore Laksa (rice noodles with coconut milk and seafood), Szechwan Black Tan Tan noodles (wide noodles, spicy meat, and cashews), and Middle Eastern tomato harissa chicken.

WHY IS THE SUNFLOWER ZAMA'S OFFICIAL FLOWER?

The sunflower is used as a "fill in" crop after the June wheat harvest. Zama has more than half-a-million sunflowers blooming along the Sagami River, and two annual sunflower festivals every summer. The flowers not only help improve soil by absorbing toxins, but they also attract pollinators — and tourists!

WHAT'S A "SCOOP CAKE"?

Scoop Cake is a popular Japanese dessert similar to British trifle, but in cake form. Topped with a decorative arrangement of white and pink grapefruit sections, this cake alternates layers of Chantilly cream and raspberry mousse, and is more delicious than you could imagine. It is also available with fresh whole strawberries. Simply scoop a serving and enjoy!

WHAT'S THE PRODUCE SELECTION LIKE AT THE ZAMA WAREHOUSE?

In addition to a wide selection of seasonal produce, there are also many kinds of fresh mushrooms, whole fresh edamame, sea asparagus, and Hokkaido fresh corn. Costco employees shuck the corn by hand and package it in plastic bags, which is unusually hands-on for the warehouse experience. [SEE "JAPAN"]

ANY NOTEWORTHY LIQUOR IN THE ZAMA COSTCO?

Zama had a three-liter bottle of Campari, which was surprisingly elegant for something that large — and really well-priced at about $90. There was also a special $200 four-liter ceramic urn of Ryukyu Awamori Mizuho sake from Okinawa, considered to be Japan's oldest distilled alcoholic beverage. Need someplace to store your fine wine? Costco sells a full size Device Style wine cellar for about $1,500, which is about 40% lower than other retailers.

ACKNOWLEDGMENTS

On Saturday, November 14, 2009 — two days after Costco opened a warehouse in Manhattan — we went out to dinner with our good friends Pat Sapinsley and Harold Levy. At dinner, Harold's friend, Simon ("Sy") Lorne, asked Susan how her day had been. She excitedly told him about our visit to the new Costco and he replied nonchalantly that he knew the founders. When Sy worked as a lawyer at Munger Tolles, he was Sol Price's lawyer, and represented Price Club during the 1993 merger with Costco. Seven years later, in August 2016, when Susan had the idea of writing a book about Costco, she remembered that conversation. We can never repay Sy for his help — especially for his generous introduction to Charlie Munger.

Warren Buffett, Charlie's longtime business partner, tells a joke about asking to be shot by hijackers before having to listen to Charlie give his talk about why he loves Costco one last time — with illustrations, no less. (Many of our friends probably feel this way about us!) We are eternally grateful to Charlie for sharing his deep knowledge of Costco with us. This book might eventually have happened without Charlie's help, but it wouldn't have been nearly as much fun.

As of May 2023, Costco had over 850 warehouses in 14 countries and 304,000 full and part-time employees. We have not yet been to all of the warehouses or spoken to every employee, but we have been to over 200 warehouses around the world and spent time with countless employees at every level of the company. We've also had a chance to visit vendors, distribution centers, and manufacturing facilities. Out of respect for Costco's humble, team-work culture, we have agreed not to thank any of the individual Costco employees or vendors who spoke to us on (or off) the record — we would like to thank them all. We hope everyone respects this difficult decision. However we would like to thank Robert Price, Mitch Lynn, Giles

Bateman, Joe Ellis, Hans Schoepflin, and Ken Chenault, none of whom work at Costco.

In November 2019, our friends Deb Futter and Bill Cohan introduced us to our literary agent, Jim Levine at Levine Greenberg Rostan. Jim and his colleague, Courtney Paganelli, are fellow Costco fans and have been vital to the project. They stood by us when we turned down both offers we received from existing publishers (22 others passed on it) and instead decided to set up our own publishing company. Not only did they edit and advise on publishing strategy, but they also recommended Bonnie Siegler, our Art Director, founder of Eight and a Half, New York. Bonnie's sense of design is unmatched, and it was a joy working with her and Andy Capelli. We were delighted when our illustrator, Martin Hargreaves, joined the Hot Dog Press team. We loved his work, which reminded us of John Tenniel; his agent, Karen Kaller, is a gem. We were thrilled that Pennie Clark Ianniciello, newly retired after 30-plus years as Costco's head book buyer, agreed to work as a consultant on the project. She may live far away, but she has always been there for us. Our copy editor, Ron Brawer, a champion senior swimmer, worked tirelessly to relocate our misplaced modifiers.

The production, sales, and distribution of the book was less daunting thanks to Ryan Whalen at Lakeside Book Company and Kevin Votel at Ingram/PGW, both of whom appreciated our passion for this project, and were so patient as we learned how to be publishers. We are grateful to both of them and to their teams. Huge thanks to David Hahn, Deb Kohan, and the gang at Finn Partners for handling our publicity.

Carolyn Levin at Miller Korzenik Sommers & Rayman, a fellow early bird, was invaluable for contracts and copy legal review, and also referred us to Stacey Grossman who handled copyright and trademark registrations. We've enjoyed working with Randy Blaustein and Virginia Farcas at R. B. Blaustein for many years; they were invaluable in the early days of setting up Hot Dog Press, LLC.

Our families and friends deserve special thanks, starting with our parents. David grew up mainly on the West Coast and his family belonged to Price Club; Susan on the East Coast, is from a Costco family. We are fortunate to have similar upbringings, though, with our parents stressing the importance of taking risks and enjoying your work. We've done both with this book. We've travelled over 200,000 miles — more than eight times around the Earth! Thanks to Larry Salamone for keeping our house plants alive while we were away. Thanks to everyone for listening to us talk about Costco with increasing passion — and in increasing detail — over the past seven years. We look forward to continuing to travel the world visiting Costco warehouses (and birding), but also to spending more time with our friends and our kids, Alex and Christy, and our two grandsons, Miles and Eli.

CREDITS

CARTOONS

PAGE 10: CARTOON BY JOE DATOR,
COURTESY OF *THE NEW YORKER* COLLECTION/THE CARTOON BANK

PAGE 69: CARTOON BY SIGNE WILKINSON,
COURTESY OF CARTOONSTOCK.COM

PAGE 202: CARTOON BY SAMMI SKOLMOSKI & SOPHIE LUCIDO JOHNSON,
COURTESY OF *THE NEW YORKER/* THE CARTOON BANK

PHOTOS

PAGES 11–13: COURTESY OF AUTHORS

PAGES 14–15: COURTESY OF COSTCO WHOLESALE CORPORATION

PAGES 16–19: COURTESY OF THE SAN DIEGO HISTORY CENTER

PAGE 20: COURTESY OF TEMPE HISTORY MUSEUM

PAGE 22: COURTESY OF ARCHIV LEBENSMITTEL ZEITUNG,
FRANKFURT, GERMANY

PAGE 23: COURTESY OF SAN DIEGO HISTORY CENTER

PAGE 24: COURTESY OF JIM COIT

PAGES 25–26: COURTESY OF COSTCO WHOLESALE CORPORATION

PAGE 28: COURTESY OF ALAMY PHOTO LIBRARY,
COPYRIGHT ROB CRANDALL

PAGE 29: COURTESY OF COSTCO WHOLESALE CORPORATION

PAGES 31–32: COURTESY OF SUSAN SCHWARTZ

PAGES 33–34: COURTESY OF COSTCO WHOLESALE CORPORATION

PAGE 35: COURTESY OF REDUX PICTURES, COPYRIGHT BEN BAKER

PAGE 36: COURTESY OF COSTCO WHOLESALE CORPORATION

PAGE 64: ILLUSTRATION BY MARTIN HARGREAVES
OF ROBERT WECHSLER'S PHOTOGRAPH OF HIS INSTALLATION
APPLIED GEOMETRY, 2004

PAGE 179: ILLUSTRATION BY MARTIN HARGREAVES
BASED ON PHOTO COURTESY OF MONICA BROSHAT

PAGE 219: ILLUSTRATION BY MARTIN HARGREAVES
BASED ON SCULPTURE BY KYUNGMIN KIM AND
PHOTO COURTESY OF SUSAN SCHWARTZ

BIBLIOGRAPHY

ARMANIOS, FEBE AND BOĞAÇ ERGENE. *HALAL FOOD: A HISTORY.*
NEW YORK: OXFORD UNIVERSITY PRESS, 2018.

KRAIG, BRUCE. *HOT DOG: A GLOBAL HISTORY.*
LONDON: REAKTION BOOKS, 2009.

PRICE, ROBERT E. *SOL PRICE: RETAIL REVOLUTIONARY & SOCIAL INNOVATOR.*
SAN DIEGO: SAN DIEGO HISTORICAL SOCIETY, 2012.

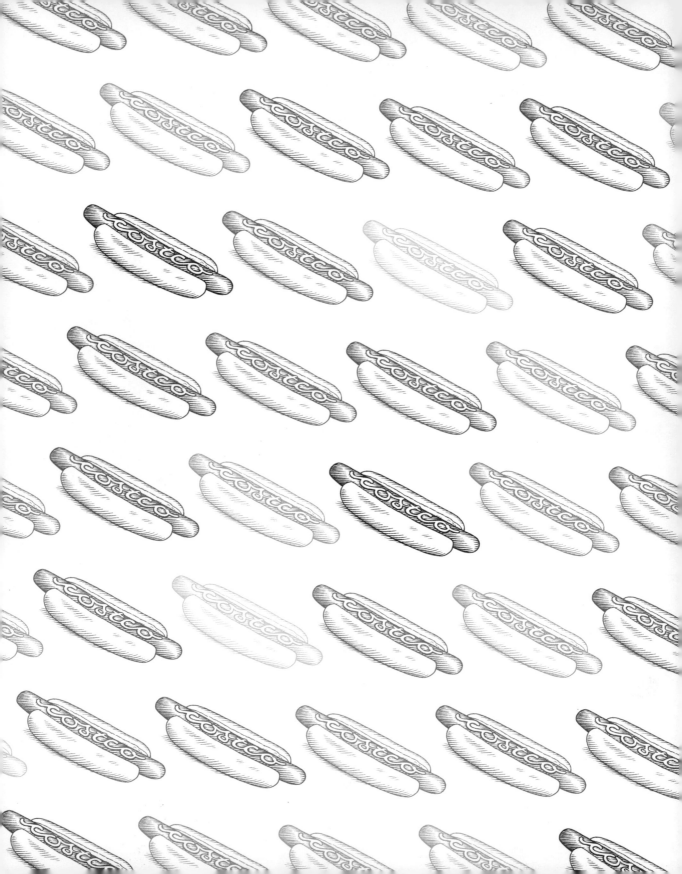